COMEBACK EVOLUTION

SERIES ON OHIO HISTORY AND CULTURE

Series on Ohio History and Culture
Kevin Kern, Editor

Russ Musarra and Chuck Ayers, *Walks Around Akron: Rediscovering a City in Transition*

Heinz Poll, edited by Barbara Schubert, *A Time to Dance: The Life of Heinz Poll*

Mark D. Bowles, *Chains of Opportunity: The University of Akron and the Emergence of the Polymer Age, 1909–2007*

Russ Vernon, *West Point Market Cookbook*

Stan Purdum, *Pedaling to Lunch: Bike Rides and Bites in Northeastern Ohio*

Joyce Dyer, *Goosetown: Reconstructing an Akron Neighborhood*

Steve Love, *The Indomitable Don Plusquellic: How a Controversial Mayor Quarterbacked Akron's Comeback*

Robert J. Roman, *Ohio State Football: The Forgotten Dawn*

Timothy H. H. Thoresen, *River, Reaper, Rail: Agriculture and Identity in Ohio's Mad River Valley, 1795–1885*

Mark Auburn, *In the President's Home: Memories of the Akron Auburns*

Brian G. Redmond, Bret J. Ruby, and Jarrod Burks, eds., *Encountering Hopewell in the Twenty-first Century, Ohio and Beyond. Volume 1: Monuments and Ceremony*

Brian G. Redmond, Bret J. Ruby, and Jarrod Burks, eds., *Encountering Hopewell in the Twenty-first Century, Ohio and Beyond. Volume 2: Settlements, Foodways, and Interaction*

Jen Hirt, *Hear Me Ohio*

Ray Greene, *Coach of a Different Color: One Man's Story of Breaking Barriers in Football*

S. Victor Fleisher, *The Goodyear Tire & Rubber Company: A Photographic History , 1898–1951*

John Tully, *Labor in Akron, 1825–1945*

Deb Van Tassel Warner and Stuart Warner, eds., *Akron's Daily Miracle: Reporting the News in the Rubber City*

Mary O'Connor, *Free Rose Light*

Walter K. Delbridge and Kate Tucker, editor, *Comeback Evolution: Selected Works of Walter K. Delbridge*

For a complete listing of titles published in the series, go to www.uakron.edu/uapress.

COMEBACK EVOLUTION

Selected Works of Walter K. Delbridge

Edited by Kate Tucker

The University of Akron Press
Akron, Ohio

ISBN: 978-1-62922-124-3 (paper)
ISBN: 978-1-62922-125-0 (ePDF)
ISBN: 978-1-62922-126-7 (ePub)

A catalog record for this title is available from the Library of Congress.

∞The paper used in this publication meets the minimum requirements of ANSI/NISO
z39.48–1992 (Permanence of Paper).

Cover image: *Guardian Queen* by Angelbert Metoyer. Courtesy of Angelbert's Imagination
Studio, used with permission.

Cover design by Amy Freels.

Comeback Evolution was designed and typeset in Minion by Amy Freels and printed on
sixty-pound white and bound by Bookmasters of Ashland, Ohio.

Produced in conjunction with the University
of Akron Affordable Learning Initiative.
More information is available at
www.uakron.edu/affordablelearning/

I am not equal to the writing, so I'll channel…

—Walter K. Delbridge

Contents

The Evolution of a Comeback   1

Fruits of Memory from the Alphabet Tree

Biography of Walter K. Dancy   17

Jazz Coltrane Sings   18

Biographical Notes: Stephen Henderson on Walter Dancy   20

Chinese River Prophet Song   21

The Metaphorical Egress   23

This the Poet as I See   24

Letter to the National Institute of Mental Health   29

Isolation and Intellect

Awakening   35

Fugue   36

Excellence   38

Cosmic Regression   39

Evaluation   40

Psychoid   41

The Mystic   42

Crystal Consciousness   43

Peregrination   44

An Artist's Soul Free and Cycling   45

Overview   47

From the Ache to the Crown   48

A Noble Fry   49

Offended Love   51

Into   52

Triumph   53

Cupid's Eagle   54

Beauty Wakes Me   55

Subtle Psychism   56

Muse Magic   57

Sleep Darling   58

Snow Crystal Flakes and Geometric Ubiquity   59

Basics   60

The Bed: Frontier of Invention   61

Nova   62

Charades   64

Past Time Games   65

To Die Unfulfilled   67

See See   69

The Will to Live as an Intuition of Purpose   70

Dialogues of Uncertainty: The Beginning of Wisdom   72

The Sage Saint in a Militaristic World   73

Spirit Fusion   74

History Lesson   75

Love General   76

Lone Wolf   77

Spells   78

Language   79

Reason's Bad Season   80

Surging Forth   81

Prayer to Earth   82

The Power of Eros   83

Soft Elegance   84

Mirrored Revelation   85

Caverns   86

Brain Chain Miracle   87

Perceptics   88

Pause in Thought   89

Gemnal Dream   90

Lyric Figures   91

Sea Scenes   92

Diamonds   94

Atlas   95
Sonics   96
Historamus   97
Volatile Silence   98
Rose Rose   99
Iris   100
Gradation   101
Bio-Mathic Reflections   102
Power Circle   103
Einstein   104
Lore   105
Energics   106
Elixir   107
The Key to Anti-Gravity is the Creative Mind   108
Sun Centers and Galactic Imagination   109
The Last Cosmocraft   110
Psi Cosmos Religion   111
Psi Master   112
Grand Architect Eternal   113
Foetal Dreams and Infinite Memories   114
Interval   116
Treasonous Reason   117
The Only Way   118
O Beautiful Spring   119
Stress View   120
Love Vertigo   121
Dove Dance   122
The Leaf Falls in Fall to Complete a Cycle   123
Olga   124
The Honeybee (for myself)   127

Once a Schizophrenic, Twice a Poet

Coordinates   133
Day Job   134
Clockwork   135

Disintegration   136
Who's on First   137
Father Forgive   138
He Who Has Ears   139
In My Hermitage   140
I Kissed a Leaf Tonight   141
Braintechtonics   142
Why I Cry   143
Peculiarity   144
The Giant   145
Utility   146
Conformity Perspective   147
Understanding Positive Mutations (Speculative Article) 148
Reprise (a poem at age 66)   150
Book of Ideas
Book of Ideas   155
Idea Roots   156
God, Musings, and Memories   159
Sun on Glass Lake   161
Moonbeam Down Sliding the Rising of Life   162
Touch Tones: Inner / Outer Working Insights:
    Neurocracy Old and New / Fragments of a Creative Path
    (May–June 2009)   166
Untitled   171
Soul Stages   173
Journal of a Reflective Poet   179

Acknowledgments   225
Notes   228
Bibliography   231

The Evolution of a Comeback

It's the evening of April 4, 1968, and news of Martin Luther King's assassination has just reached Atlanta. Students flood the campus of Morehouse College—Dr. King's alma mater—angry, heartbroken, afraid. Sophomore class president Walter Dancy addresses the crowd, urging them to remember Dr. King's legacy of nonviolence. The next morning, they take to the streets, where Dancy and another Morehouse student convince the mayor to let them march peacefully. In the following days, Dancy and fellow classmate Samuel L. Jackson become embroiled in tensions in the Black Freedom Movement. Jackson is expelled for protesting, and Dancy doesn't finish the semester. He returns to school the following year but continues to spiral as he struggles to support his mother and seven siblings with his scholarship money.

In December 1969, he is drafted. During his intake, the Army psychiatrist says to him: "I hear you think you'll be studied in American Literature one day?" Dancy answers affirmatively and the psychiatrist makes his diagnosis: "Here is a twenty-three-year-old Black man who claims to understand complex subjects and thinks he will be studied in American Literature. Orientation good. Judgment impaired. Diagnosis paranoid schizophrenic."[1] Having previously attended Harvard and Yale, Dancy had just been awarded a prestigious scholarship to study at the Sorbonne, but he would not make the journey to Paris.

Instead, Dancy returns home to Akron, where he's taken by police to Fallsview Psychiatric Hospital. While institutionalized, his poetry is published in Orde Coombs' critically acclaimed anthology *We Speak as Liberators*, but he will not discover this until 2019, nearly fifty years later. Heavy medication obliterates his memory until he is no longer president of Garfield High's class of '65, National Urban League Student President, lead actor in the legendary Morehouse-Spelman Players, editor-in-chief of the *Morehouse Tiger*, illustrious Charles Merrill Scholar, star breadwinner and guiding light in a family of nine. From his shoulders the whole world falls, as with Atlas in a poem Dancy would later rise to write:

> And yet he trembles at the thought
> A noble act or just aching muscles
> Made him loose the world
> Whether his spirit lagged
> Or the pain of labor pried his fingers loose
> Or did sleep overcome his resolution?
>
> He watches the earth fall yet
> He
> Was too much to dwell within it:
> > His shadow the night
> > His eyes
> > The sun and moon

By the time Dancy's poetry is published a second time, in a prominent anthology alongside Langston Hughes, Lead Belly, Gwendolyn Brooks, and Audre Lorde, he is working at Akron General Hospital as a dishwasher, occasionally delivering meals to patients. The *Akron Beacon Journal*, which had reported Dancy's achievements from junior high school onward, breaks its streak of laudatory coverage without a word. While his peers go on to be successful doctors, lawyers, and Hollywood actors, Dancy falls behind and becomes, as he would later say, "stuck in the system ever since."

Three years after the fateful diagnosis, Dancy makes a quiet return to his studies, earning a BA in English Literature from The University of Akron. In a metamorphic move, he changes his name from his mother's maiden name Dancy to his father's surname Delbridge, effectively cutting ties with his past life and from anyone who would look for the rising star in him, including the literary critics writing of his work.[2]

He is offered a graduate fellowship at The University of Akron, but in his first year of teaching, his brother Willie is murdered. Delbridge leaves the program and spends the next decade in and out of psych wards, living a life of relative isolation. Later recounting this time, he says, "Regardless of what we could have been, we are what we are within."

In April 1979, during what he describes as an incredible period of enlightenment, Delbridge pens a cycle of 133 poems in under twenty-four hours to a soundtrack of Coltrane and Mingus. He calls it *Isolation and Intellect.* With themes ranging from love to alienation, disability to remarkability, these poems offer a unique glimpse into the mind of a man struggling to regain his voice. However, it would take many years for the poetry to reach beyond the isolation of Delbridge's own life.

THE COMEBACK

In 2002, I met Walter Delbridge. My truck driver dad had struck up a friendship on the loading dock of Borders Books and Music with an employee who took his lunch breaks outside to avoid his racist coworkers. As my dad made his regular deliveries, he and Walter exchanged books, ideas, personal stories, and laughter. While I was home for Christmas, Walter came over for dinner, and when he learned I was a songwriter, he asked if I would look at his poetry. He told me he'd been writing under the influence of jazz. "Maybe you could find some inspiration for your music."

I returned to Seattle with a box full of cigar-tinged manuscripts and began what would become a long and ever-deepening collaboration with Walter Delbridge. I started by transcribing his handwritten pages to digital form, a process I continue to this day. As I came to see the rhythm and jazz-poetry of his voice, I longed to know more about *him.* What kind of life would inform such a uniquely focused and yet utterly wide-open vision?

We became friends. I called him for advice, even during my divorce. I visited him whenever I was home, and my parents became closer with him too, my mother turning to him for help through her depression. When she died, Walter sat next to my dad at the funeral.

Eventually, I asked if he would allow me to submit his work to be published, and in the process of discovering Delbridge's poetic voice, I came to know the man who could channel such variegated emotion and spin it into song, even the most disparate of tones. I knew that other people would want to know him too. With his permission, I began to record our conversations, and that led to the idea of a documentary film, now nearing completion. As the camera focused, he revealed layer after layer of spirit and depth.

Delbridge gave his first poetry reading to a sold-out crowd at the 2017 Rubber City Jazz and Blues Festival. He opened his performance by stating, "I am not equal to the writing, so I'll channel..." and he brought down the house. He's been invited to return every year. In 2019, Delbridge was the featured guest at Art of Recovery in Akron's historic Greystone Hall, and at E. J. Thomas Hall he read his poetry to the tune of Theron Brown and his jazz quartet performing music inspired by Delbridge's work. Of late, he has more invitations than he can accept. To this he says, "The body is aging, while the mind and spirit brighten."

One invitation Delbridge has sought his entire life is to be published. Unaware that his earlier poems had been published in the seventies, he did not enjoy this achievement until Oxford University Press published two of his poems, along with a letter he wrote to the National Institute of Mental Health in the May 2017 issue of their prominent journal *Schizophrenia Bulletin*. Still, he dreamed of a collection that would expand on the inner dialogue he'd begun in *Isolation and Intellect*, inviting others to join the conversation.

Here we arrive full circle at what can be held within the pages of a book—a whole life's resolution, hope, and subsequent discipline come to consummation against terrible odds and repeated injustice. We see "an artist's soul, free and cycling," beyond any stigmatic label, system of oppression, or denial of resource; this poetry a coding, a neural network of truth and beauty, survival and strength. As Delbridge describes it, "I decided to steel my mind, build a coding within myself, a flexible coding inside my body and keep building on it. You have to strive for a quiet mind that you can turn in any direction."

CODING

Delbridge's approach to survival through mindfulness and creative generation could be seen as Afrofuturistic. The building of a mind of steel with an internal coding to protect himself from all manner of threats recalls the inner worlds Octavia Butler so deftly created. As with Butler, Delbridge's work extends beyond the frame of a sci-fi futurism as he reclaims a past erased and reconstructs a future based on that reimagined past. Suffering from amnesia surrounding the time of his greatest achievement, he is forced to recreate his past from fragmented memories constantly contested by a system which seeks to explain his experience in short and deadly labels like "schizophrenic," "poor," and "black." Thus, he becomes as Sam Riddell describes, "caught in the ironic crossroads of being hyper visible and invisible."[3] The words of Sun Ra in the film *Space Is the Place* could be Delbridge's own:

> I'm not real, I'm just like you. You don't exist in this society. If you did, your people would not be seeking equal rights. You're not real. If you were, you'd have some status among the nations of the world. [...] I do not come to you as a reality, I come to you as a myth because that's what black people are: myths. I come from a dream that the black man dreamed long ago.[4]

Author and filmmaker Ytasha Womack writes in *Afrofuturism: The World of Black Sci-Fi and Fantasy Culture* that Afrofuturists are free to do what they want, and their expressions are uniquely individual, as Afrofuturism doesn't create in opposition to anything. "Self-expression in Afrofuturism isn't about making a statement, it's about being."[5] Being was all that was left for Delbridge to do. In a sense, he lived in the vacuum of his otherness, initially sent there against his will but ultimately transformed by his own choosing to exist in spite of the oppression that could deny even his life. There is a resonance in a history that has been drowned and then resuscitated by a reclamation of agency over one's story, a story that has been co-opted and psychologically manipulated by an official culture rooted in white supremacy.

In *We Speak as Liberators,* the first book to feature Delbridge's poetry, published in 1970 while he was institutionalized, editor Orde Coombs refers to the psychological three times in the brief introduction:

> ...For it was clear to me that we were faced with a generation of black writers who had decided that, at whatever cost, they would psychologically liberate themselves from the altar of white supremacy....
> ...Symbols of white psychological rule that have emblazoned the earth....And it is here too, that they find the genesis of the lies that were cruelly meant to keep us—forever—in psychological bondage.

Evidence for white supremacy as institutionalized psychological bondage can be seen in the American Psychiatric Association's 1968 decision to change the definition of schizophrenia. The second edition of their *Diagnostic and Statistical Manual*, still regarded as the bible of psychiatry in its updated fifth edition, recast the paranoid aspect of schizophrenia as a disorder of masculinized belligerence, expressed in "frequently hostile and aggressive" behavior.[6] Overnight, schizophrenia became the diagnosis of choice to levy against Black men participating in the civil rights movement, psychiatrist and Vanderbilt University professor Jonathan Metzl asserts, so much so that doctors would come to call it protest psychosis.[7]

"By definition, schizophrenia is a diagnosis of exclusion: Clinicians must rule out other potential causes of symptoms, including mood disorders, before the diagnosis of schizophrenia is given," says Michael Gara, professor of psychiatry at Rutgers Robert Wood Johnson Medical School. But where *exclusion* should work in one's favor, preventing a hasty and ill-informed diagnosis, for Black Americans, it is more likely to manifest as exclusion *from* society, with studies continuing to show a bias in misdiagnosing Black Americans with schizophrenia.[8] Whether or not Delbridge had schizophrenia at the time of his diagnosis, we'll never know, but what we do know is how the system responded to him as soon as he got caught up in it.

In the sixties, the United States military was sending disproportionate numbers of Black men to fight on the front lines in Vietnam,[9] and if they didn't make it that far, committing them to the 1960's equivalent of the prison industrial complex—the mental institution—never to be heard from again.[10] Young Black leaders rose only to their peril, catching the attention of J. Edgar Hoover and COINTELPRO, who would run them into exile or worse. Samuel L. Jackson recounts his expulsion from Morehouse and involvement with the Black Power movement: "All of a sudden, I felt I had a voice. I was somebody. I could make a difference. But then one day, my mom showed up and put me on a plane to LA. She said, 'Do not come back to Atlanta.' The FBI had been to the house and told her that if I didn't get out of Atlanta, there was a good possibility I'd be dead within a year."[11]

Delbridge has stated that J. Edgar Hoover was after him, and what-
ever went down, he went down headfirst with it, though he refused the
mantle of civil rights leader and resisted the pull of Black Power politics.[12]
He once declined an invitation to the White House to represent the
National Urban League, procured by prominent civil rights leader and
March on Washington organizer Whitney Young Jr. Still, Delbridge's
poetic vision and general philosophy on life ring true to Coombs'
framing of radical Black literary voices: "One finds the sustained passion,
the uncompromising necessity to affirm, to safeguard, a dignity so long
denied. And the blackness, always the attempt to turn what was once
negative into a sharpening rod of creativity."

"THE LYRICISTS TURNED INWARD . . ."

The sharpening rod of creativity leads to transcendence for Delbridge,
who asserts he was not commenting on Black struggle, but rather on
human experience on a spiritual level. Upon reading Professor Kimberly
Benston's analysis of Delbridge's poem "Jazz Coltrane Sings" in his book
Performing Blackness: Enactments of African-American Modernism,
Delbridge says:

> It's interesting, but he misses my intent in writing the poem in the first
> place. Absorption and the changes and the richness of the music itself,
> the richness of the tonality changes, the richness from "Ballads" to
> "Bessie's Blues," to "Om" and "Expressions" and "Nature Boy" and all
> those songs. I was absorbing his music, music as a spiritual emotion,
> immersed in the whole atmosphere of his music, recognizing the spir-
> ituality of the man through his music, most of it a spiritual version of
> his emotions. I didn't get into all the politics of Black and White
> dynamics. [Benston's] proposition seems to be political, he's thinking
> in terms of Black struggle, Black identity, and so on. I'm thinking of
> universal experience, of the spiritual, and the soul experience of taking
> participation in a great artist's music.

At age seventy-three, Delbridge's response to Benston is fully aligned
with his twenty-three-year-old self who writes for his brief author's bio
in *We Speak as Liberators*: "I feel that life is music given flesh." Delbridge
does not skirt issues of Blackness, nor does he refuse to acknowledge the
effects of systemic racism—quite the contrary. He does, however, seek

"a higher plane" where all intersections of oppression are transcended, all the while celebrating the human on its way to the divine. He is most in line with Coombs' observation: "The lyricists turned inward, not in defeat, but in celebration of what was always there..."

In a manifesto-like piece, "This the Poet as I See," published in the formidable anthology by Stephen Henderson, *Understanding the New Black Poetry: Black Speech and Black Music as Poetic References,* Delbridge writes:

> A poet is a mind sailor soul dweller and teller of heartbeats. The infinite is the galaxies of his pulse and his soul is a chamber orchestra of endless incantations. [...] he is a listener of voices, a reader of lips and a vocalist of myriad dreams. He is colors spread like light through a prism and like sand transmuted to silicone glinting of glass. [...] Black is beautiful true like all shades of Nature with potential beauty when the snow-blind melts from our eyes. A verse framer or rime dodger when the subject calls for blank conversing he is a maker of soul magic and a stroker of the mysterious cat who lives in our dreamy dark called living. A poet I see must be the me in all of we and nature and life eternal screaming and praying and saying—tell it like it is.

Afrosurrealism describes an arts movement popularized by D. Scot Miller in 2009 in his famous "Afrosurreal Manifesto," first printed in the *San Francisco Bay Guardian.* Unlike Afrofuturism, Afrosurrealism is concerned with the present, or the future-past which is "RIGHT NOW," directly where Delbridge finds himself in "This the Poet as I See," telling it like it is. The present is a multi-dimensional space allowing the poet to move from visible to invisible, with the mandate that he discover or uncover the "galaxies of his pulse," no matter if this appears as "madness." The Afrosurrealist recognizes madness as visitation from the gods, an acknowledgement of the possibility of magic. D. Scot Miller writes, "We take up the obsessions of the ancients and kindle the dis-ease, clearing the murk of the collective unconsciousness as it manifests in these dreams called culture."[13]

Afrofuturist experience and Afrosurreal expression meet in Delbridge's work, where "he is a maker of soul magic and a stroker of the mysterious cat who lives in our dreamy dark called living." Is this Schrödinger's cat? The cat whose life and death depend upon our observation of it, whose past and future live in a space of truth and fiction as in the Afrofuturistic reimagination? The cat is alive and well in Delbridge's manifesto, though cloistered in a dreamy darkness. If no one can see it, the cat is not forced to collapse into one reality, to be declared living or dead. This collapsing into a single reality is one of the biggest quandaries of quantum physics, and of the schizophrenic mind. In an Afrosurreal sense, myriad possibilities exist within a parallel multiverse. The one who observes is observed and on we go into higher consciousness.

It's one thing to distort reality as a device for emotional impact in the creation of artistic work, it's a whole other thing to struggle to grasp a consensus reality that makes up the framework of society, a reality that is threatened by real mental illness and the drugs that come with it. Regardless of what caused what—the "madness," the poetry, the illness, the poison cure of pharmaceuticals, the exile—Delbridge experienced the enforced denial and subsequent distortion of his own individual reality by both the white establishment and by his own community.

Delbridge's willingness to express unfiltered the emotional impact of his lived experience is what could place him within the landscape of Afrosurrealism. In a 2020 interview, Delbridge cited "neglect" as the kindest word he could use to describe the way the Black community treated him upon his release.[14] He is telling it like it is for better or worse, his mental health diagnosis slapped like police tape across the door of his "hermitage."

> In my hermitage I think not brood
> What good to brood over life full of surprises
> Best to enjoy Fate and fulfilled destiny
> [...]
> While I'm in solitude
> There are young minds
> Sometimes in old bodies
> Questioning and questioning for new ways to live
> In my hermitage I listen to music, I read books
> And live a full life with myself
> My true joys cannot be condensed to a small quotation
> My anguish cannot be compressed into a mere complaint

Delbridge is living beyond classification here in the Afrosurrealist way, moving freely among alias, defying census, refusing to identify with any one discipline, calling, or name. Safe within his hermitage, he frequently changes his phone number and maintains no email address. This way of life, though chosen to some degree by Delbridge after its initial imposition via forced institutionalization, reflects a disconnection from community and Black culture in particular, a fight-or-flight reaction to living in a collectively anti-Black American society. We don't yet know whether his work ought to be placed within Afrofuturism or Afrosurrealism, or somewhere else entirely. He remains outside, as he writes in the poem "Peculiarity:"

> He was such a rarity
> That one day while he was away
> Someone put a "For Sale" sign
> On his door
>
> Strange:
> He bought it.

We too have bought some form of this—book, line, and story. For various reasons, no doubt, we may see ourselves in Delbridge. We may at the same time wonder if his words are true; we may test what we perceive as his reality against the unsettling diagnosis of schizophrenia. A student intern from Vanderbilt University working on the Walter Delbridge documentary wrote a letter to Delbridge revealing that she was drawn to his work because some of her family members have schizophrenia. He wrote back:

Schizophrenia seems to be nature's way of trying to make AM into FM, or a DVD into an all-purpose entertainment center. It's a way of playing on the senses. It's a way of nature trying to get the whole nervous system online with all the separate parts working as one concerted unit.

In the beginning there's a division, there may be several voices within one's voice, there may be several consciousnesses within one's own consciousness, but eventually the whole purpose is to become totally unified and act as one organism, one mind with many variations within that mind. It's an attempt of nature to produce a more complex, but more integrated being.

Now most people who are normal, they have gotten their socialization, they fit into the pattern of the social system, they fit into a neat box, they allow themselves to be pigeonholed; whereas in the so-called schizophrenic, you have a person who finds it difficult to fit into the pigeonholes because that person is using more of their mind.

It may be awkward in a way because so much data is coming at them within, so many pictures, ideas, movies, memories, that they may seem distracted or overly intense, but that's all a matter of pacing and in due time, with the right kind of training, they can become more unified, more careful, more succinct, more direct, more powerful as a communicator and as an existent being. This is all part of that journey.

I'd like to know where your relatives are on that journey so I can either say something, or stand back and admire and listen and respect life, because this far exceeds what any of us know. Life far exceeds anything any of us know. We are always progressing and learning in this area and unfortunately the experts themselves, many of them have stopped learning. They stopped with their dissertation or with their professor's dissertation. Some of us are condemned to keep learning because we have the condition. I will try to make the most of it.

With Delbridge, we are invited to make the most of it, to stand back in awe of that which far exceeds what any of us know. In a moment of foreshadowing just before his diagnosis, Delbridge wrote in *We Speak as Liberators,* "Imagination is most real for seeing possibilities that limited reality excludes. Am curious to understand the entire universe and mirror it in poetry." The scales were already falling from his eyes. To understand the universe, a lofty goal. But who could resist a look into that mirror?

Kate Tucker, April 2021

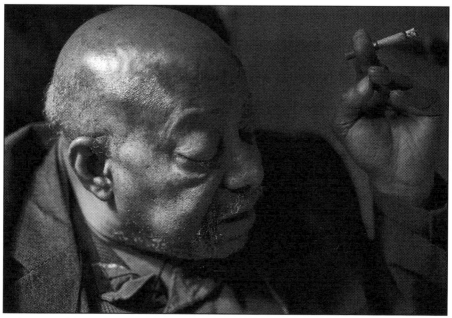

Walter K. Delbridge. *Photo by Miriam Bennett.*

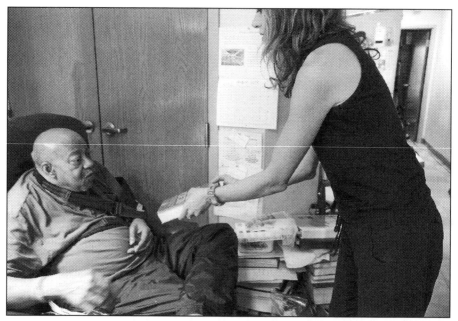

Kate Tucker gives Walter Delbridge a book containing poems he'd written in college. He had never seen them in published form. *Photo by Miriam Bennett.*

Delbridge looks for his lost poems, never having seen them in print. *Photo by Cameron Kaglic.*

Delbridge discovering his own poetry again. *Photo by Cameron Kaglic.*

Fruits of Memory from the
Alphabet Tree

Biography of Walter K. Dancy[15]

Born in April 24, 1946 (Taurus)
fourth of eight children
Father played guitar and sang blues
Mother an excellent story-teller
Neither finished grade school
I feel that life is music given flesh. All life interest—pain, beauty, struggle
Imagination is most real for seeing possibilities that limited reality excludes.
Am curious to understand the entire universe and mirror it in poetry.

Jazz Coltrane Sings

Like one of my professors said to me
some hep cat with soul in his pen or type should write
a jazz
po
em o
baby don't you weep cause
I's here and the
music of Train is
blowing
showing all
the colors spread in OM
with Expression crying a
LOVE Supreme on screeching
Meditations
Chim Chim Chereeing over
Nature Boy's last solo
while Elvin is sweating over
Bessie's Blues
he can't get away from the
Father
the Son and
all are Holy with the Ghost
singing A Love Supreme and
doing Dahomey's Dance
can you hear
can you hear
can you hear
the real McCoy
Tyner touching those ivory keys
and Train

Train is blowing all the colors in OM
saying
MOM HOME WOMB TOMB soon like
a crazy spiritual fly away home

Train is gone

        gone

            gone

                baby don't you weep

like he's paying dues for us all
when he sings
        A LOVE SUPREME
      a love supreme
      a love supreme

      a love supreme

Biographical Notes: Stephen Henderson on Walter Dancy[16]

Walter Dancy was born in Tuskegee, Alabama,[17] and grew up in Akron, Ohio. He attended Morehouse College until he was forced to leave because of ill health. A brilliant, original student with a wide range of interests including mathematics, science, philosophy, and literature, his poems in this volume have not been previously published.

Chinese River Prophet Song

Over the Yellow River and Canton
and the muddy Ganges
Times will like Gandhi's be gone over to
ideas with condition red

ideas live
echoing for centuries
now they too are subject to sudden death

Religion will swell the awing waters
of the world when only one nation
rules
When only one nation can be right and
white
then the world will glow with atomic
light to make bright the genocidal night
to teach those once and for all in darkness

Frail we cringe before Dante's Italic vision
its cineramic focus and panavision scale
swells brain-mind to deluxe colored
shell of skull holding vision and
an incision in our dreams heal
not with the words of the drunk
surgeon leader
dipping and ripping brains bathed in
the gun fluids of war

Not ready for peace
the lump of mud in our souls
resists reason competing with screaming howls
a monkey in tuxedo with tails
without a tail
we tear ourselves away from ideals
slobbering spit-mouths of threats

Like ocean spray mist flying our
hope on the wind blowing from the sea side
at high tide all is muggy and hot with fear
are we ill?

Or is the pride of reckoning for ourselves real?

The sun set sinking in the old man's eyes
the yellow burns with a tinge of sun-red glow

The child smiles before the coming locusts
seventeen years hungry
thinking them pretty in
the wild swaying wheat

Metaphors devour reality making real the unseen
but dimly felt—making felt in full the threshold
touch the floor never permanent the volcano's
rumbling unceasing

Dante raves under our quivering minds
China's earth is yellow underfoot.

The Metaphorical Egress

The metaphor writhes and twists seeking some meaning
in its dance around the mind
and we find hanging loose
the choice to choose or lose the pungency
of the words or fall
fumbling
after
connotations
and bruise our ankles on denotations
only
to lose the point
as our hearts become simply
blood pumps and our brains cushions
to protect our skulls from content
a metaphor is writhing struggling to be born
foetal, kicking and wanting to break the sac
wanting to breathe
into the world
a wail
singing:

Tired am I from struggle's womb
gloom dooms me to cool tears
filling the pools of my sorrow
tomorrow is the year of my sun
today is the year peace flew away in the beak of an eagle
yesterday my existence was a rehearsal of a dream
waking my sorrow gains my vision of joy
weeds choke the meadowlark destroying my youth.

This the Poet as I See

A poet is a mind sailor soul dweller and teller of heartbeats. The infinite is the galaxies of his pulse and his soul is a chamber orchestra of endless incantations. He is a voyager on an endless journey as far as the mind can race on the arrows of light and the soul can feel like morning glories greeting the rising sun. The poet is a man of all life like the timeless Llama of Legend Tibet, he is a listener of voices, a reader of lips and a vocalist of myriad dreams. He is colors spread like light through a prism and like sand transmuted to silicone glinting of glass. He is a searcher in the mystic deep, an author of the commonplace, an explorer of dim unrealized feeling. This is the way I see the sea and the way to see I with eye beyond infra-red and we all cyclic part of life, life from the widow's kiss to the electron quiver colorless but for the perishing and change. Black is beautiful true like all shades of Nature with potential beauty when the snow-blind melts from our eyes. A verse framer or rime dodger when the subject calls for blank conversing he is a maker of soul magic and a stroker of the mysterious cat who lives in our dreamy dark called living. A poet I see must be the me in all of we and nature and life eternal screaming and praying and saying—tell it like it is.

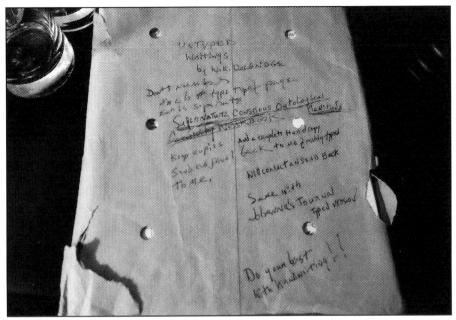

Handwritten manuscripts given by Walter Delbridge to Kate and Joanna Tucker. *Photo by Kate Tucker.*

Delbridge's writing desk with a typed draft of *Isolation and Intellect. Photo by Kate Tucker.*

Delbridge's bedroom, where he rarely sleeps. *Photo by Kate Tucker.*

Delbridge in his home in Akron. *Photo by Kate Tucker.*

Letter to the National Institute of Mental Health

Dear Sirs,

Because my experiences have been so wide, deep, and various and sometimes involved seemingly outright paranormal experiences, I have seriously doubted my own sanity for different periods of my life.

I have suffered since 1970, various diagnoses, with catatonic schizophrenia, paranoid schizophrenia, manic depressive psychosis, depressive disorder, bipolar disorder, anxiety prone personality, and currently schizoaffective disorder depressive type.

Sirs, I want you to know that while experiencing all of these illnesses, I maintained a steady state of lucidity. Even though my thoughts may have seemed disordered, I remember what I was experiencing during each of these illnesses. I have gone through some of the elements of the Freudian, Jungian, Adlerian, Existential, Reality Therapy, and other traditions in psychotherapy's symptomology.

As of 1973, a year after I left graduate school at The University of Akron, Dr. Primativa Ong of the now-defunct Fallsview Psychiatric Hospital, took my case. At this Cuyahoga Falls Ohio hospital, Dr. Ong had Dr. Susan Kaplan give me an entire battery of tests including IQ tests. She had me bring in all my writings at the time. She conducted a thorough bio-history and psychiatric interview, and she questioned me about theories that I held about reality. Dr. Ong later called me in and asked me the question: "Walter, what do you think your IQ is?" I answered that I believed it to be 150. Dr. Ong said: "No, no Walter. Do not tell anybody I told you this, they'll hate you, but your IQ is in excess of 200."

In the last two years, I was sent to a counseling psychologist who claims that my IQ is below average. After reading this material that I'm presenting to you and all of the records you can call up, sirs, you be the judge. All I can say is that I have an unusual heredity and very complicated social history involving numerous interest groups and pressure groups putting the squeeze on me my most of my life.

I'm fortunate to be able to explain this much, considering the amount of conflict that other people have brought into my existence and the discrimination and oppression that society has levered on me. Many with the same configuration would be blithering mad right now, unable to function. I am trying to find my place amidst a whole society afflicted by numerous illnesses, prejudices, dysfunction, unrealistic expectations, and denial of value to individuals who differ at all from the norm.

I have dedicated my life to the arts and sciences, striving for a quiet mind that I can turn in any direction. During one especially heightened state, I was listening to Mingus and Coltrane and began to write what would become a 133-poem cycle titled *Isolation and Intellect*. This was written over a period of twenty-four hours. I submit these poems for your examination and study, hoping that you may be able to help guide and possibly hear and understand those of us who are creative and yet are diagnosed as seriously mentally ill with the stigma and disadvantages and anguish that not only the illnesses have given us, but all the social and economic disadvantages going with it.

Sincerely,
Walter K. Delbridge

Walter Delbridge recounts his story to Joanna Tucker for the documentary *Tell It Like It Is*. *Photo by Kate Tucker.*

Delbridge's typewriter. *Photo by Miriam Bennett.*

Joanna Tucker with a stack of newly discovered manuscripts given to her by Delbridge. *Photo by Kate Tucker.*

Attempting to decipher Delbridge's journals, handwritten on graph paper. *Photo by Kate Tucker.*

Isolation and Intellect

Awakening

Immersed in Life
To see and feel Beauty out of confusion
Precious illusions gone in the face of Truth
The soul set free
Soars from constraint
Above accidental election of society

Entering subtle regions of sensibility
New sensations arrive
New seminal spiritings of mind and heart
Eager ever for rhythm and measure
Art music and romance's pleasure
Women wine and stellar tones
Time with friends and time alone
The sensuous flow of feeling
Geometric cones of thought and
Works creative carefully wrought
With all communications full of meaning
Undulating above and below through words
A rich totalistic rapture of being whole
Body and soul free streaming unity
Bold leaps of the imagination
In and out convention's domain
All this a new beginning born from pain
The ascetic starts to live again.

Fugue

As my dreams come to light
I wonder at the medallion of knowledge
Tempting me to the Nobel Prize of longing
Only to look at the Swedish girls
Wash their ears and watch illusions
That is Hiroshima mushromovies of the mind
Blown massaging the eyes

Shakespeare returns as a leprosarian beggar
Is hired by the New York Times as a copy reader
Who dreams of Avon soap and sips English tea
They took him away mad as a walrus choking
To ski or not to flee that is the answer
Ours is a logical age
No room for genius
There is normality or madness

Eighty years ago when Albert Einstein had a vision
Physics turned unguessably ghostly
The certain was a special case
And the dogmatist was out of his mind
Einstein dreamed of heaven free from time
For this glimpse of Eternity nothing is final

Change and progress are in and hippies cavalcade
And promenade and fat-cat-daddy execs send
Those checks to Sally and Joe who've gone to pot
And daddy's dreams have gone up in smoke

Magic is loose in the world
An artist's neck's in the noose in this world
Scientists say how real is the world
Politicians divide the world
Dreams are out of this world

"The Earth is the Lord's and the fullness thereof..."
Went ding dong down with the sinking of the Lusitania
The boogie-woogie's still playing in Harlem
And folks still looking for pots of gold at
The end of the rainbow despite what physicists say

The only way to make it all make sense is
With a musical instrument
And a crazy muse.

Excellence

The crowd's fickle applause or censure
Move me not
I speak to those who fritter not life and time
I've my own goals despite weal or woe
I commit myself to excellence
Self-development and wholeness

Whether seen or not
All that one's surely got
Is the true inner self
Most have surrendered to societal sham
In a rush they run to Bible, Veda, or Koran
Realizing their sin against the inner light
Takes so many years for fools to know
The outer show is just a dead hand across the path of the soul

Incidental or necessary
An automaton arrangement for convenience
Egotist! they shout
Let them shout from falsity's surface
Individual respect no doubt

When a man stops pandering to the mob
He's thrown on his own resources
To miserably fail or
Achieve golden spiritual heights
To assay truthfully issues of day and night
Either o'erwhelmed by mass might
Or reaching for divinity's
Light.

Cosmic Regression

This concentrated love bound
Round a core of aloneness
Yet spirit informs this apartness
No angel yet relieves the spiral
Into the realms of Life

Few yet have approached this core of self
Without meeting enshrouded mystery
A mystery of multifarious depth
Such aloofness is the effect of realization
Such realization leaves only Faith
An antidote to knowledge
Which binds the heart
Experiencing too much too deep too soon
A terrible knowledge which burns all illusions
Like the Grand Phoenix's feathers fired to ashes
Ashes fall away as new illusions
Fill the temporary void
Left by sudden loss of too cherished dreams

Smiling faces mock my pinched brow
Laughing mouths mock my sad eyes
And I
Filled with a cosmic horror
Shake inwardly at their unknowing innocence
For knowing makes me silent
And silence makes me aware of their momentary happiness
Knowledge not happiness drives me on
Seeing possibilities manifest before I can speak
Thought dumb in the talkative crowd

With soul full of unspeakable awareness
I speed home to sleep and retreat
From laughers and joygathers
Unmindful of Death and the poignant
Short time for facing Deity.

Evaluation

Frail webbings of illusions surround me;
What am I to do?
Shall I say age old legends are true?
Me with a surgical mind
Speeding up an incline of rigor.
Myths, true enough, have vigor
Damn! Once, twice, trice
Error too gathers apostles and
Furthermore
My mind wants no more lies
Comforting or not.
Rather I'd like to like fables
But given to penetration
I'd not be pathic to rugose fallacies;
Manly then, let the glacial vision rise
And serpentine, let the oracle indict
The age in lands far from Eden;
Let the old center eye lift its lid
To see a reality without apology:

    A spawn of hosannas halt not
    The pain in my side
    Given by surgeons of the flesh
    When I was fresh in youth
    And even the prayers are null and void
    To stop the apocryphal pain
    Gone to metaphysical misery.

Psychoid

Seeming events breaking causal rules
Psychic pranks sometimes cruel

Fiction that insures future science
Dreams grafting their way to reality
The most precious find
God deep in the mind
Loving a buxom woman several times
As distance falls to insignificance
Her sex puts a hex on my sleep
Vision too deep for explanation
Snap of insight during a nap
Evading any psychological trap
A glass which unaccountably fell
Narrating an old tale
Three pennies in an artesian well

In spring I see many things
Drink water from mountain springs
My own ghost gave a toast
To the miracle
Of double placement.

The Mystic

Stood he tall
On the high arching hill
In the bright
Moon illumined night

His soul leaped out to the
Myriad life of the aeon-existing stars
His inward being merged more and more
With Spirit-infused Nature
Radiant and triumphant in
All directions.

Crystal Consciousness

To see bright sharp and clear
The dewy rose in dawn spread morn
Live courageous and without fear
To stifle a trifle tear and stand steadfast when danger's near
The goal of the artistic seer
Wisdom and love in a sensual heat of joy

Eye trained like a spear of sunlight
Spotting insincerity in a mistress's face
Ear clear like clarion toned instrument
Hearing the subtlety in a friend's compliment
All vulgarity an offense to taste
Using the King's English without halt or haste
Sensitive to mood and muscle
Catching her desirous eye and flex of thigh

He makes rubies of experience
Learning from mistakes long gone by
And diamonds of loves lost
Recalling every pleasing detail in vivid warmth
This is crystal clear to those who can
Clearly see and clearly hear.

Peregrination

Through many diverse paths
Wend a fate
Through many an episode to the main theme
Architecting reality from a dream
Surveying immense vistas and multi-hued scenes
Screening out the vulgar dross
Refinement in time in Value's retort
Soul spun gold an immeasurable treasure

While the noise of the crowd fades
Into the arcane the quester wades
Wonders in spiralic tension
While consciousness pursues its ascension

Beyond the lure of daily inanities
And proverbial profanities
The elixir of illumination beckons

The heady mood goes on
While the soul expands its cone
There are others
We're not alone.

An Artist's Soul Free and Cycling

Concentrating on eccentric minor themes
She missed the melody of my life...

Argonaut of the Imagination! Mathematician of the Spirit!
Mind sweeper of magnetized ideas into discovery clusters
Winging bald eagle at circling heights
Metaphors unlimited
Instructed in the school of life
Empathetic rush with past Great Spirits

Leonardo's multifarious mastery secreted for years
Goethe's Olympian depth
Nietzsche's tragedy and sublime vision
Mendeleev's chemic divisions
Prophet weepers incantate the arc curve of
Riemann's non-Euclidean universe
Broken Edgar Allen Poe in a hearse
Tycho Brahe's bladder with beer did burst
Savonarola on Botticelli put a fanatic curse
And worse, exile excommunication and stake

In these giants we see
Science finds art a mirror-image of self
Ego lost in impersonal creation
Giants wade into primal waters of originality
Where egocentrated dwarfs would drown
Where the named giants in history found renown
Many vulgar rhymesters think they're great
With the applause of decadents and clowns
Justice after a moment covers their act in obscurity
And their vain egos whirl off toward offended pride
Their productions pitiful next a Shakespeare sonnet
Yet they clamor for award and publication
Concentrating on smallness, spite, and the obscene
Enough to make any real artist scream

The real artist follows the higher law where
The Creator taking myriad forms
And losing no time building patterns on the
Book of the World, ad infinitum
The Teacher brings the soul alive
Awake to the potential efflorescence of Realization.

Overview

Too late or too soon in this world
Of the whirl of groups
I spin off alone
Thoughts out of key or on the obscure
The group cannot enure
The sublime and fearsome has allure
Only for the adamant seeker
Such behavior's out of what's called style
Dirt filth and guile
Newspapers
Leave the poet poised on non-welcome
He's left to Beauty's contemplation
The coloratura of dreams and issues of feeling
Cycles of fate and things with no date
Nothing to contribute to conversation
Themselves in a circle
His long voice must reach
The lone ear
While alien to ready acceptance
His glance must be steady with mind calm
While the group haggles on a qualm.

From the Ache to the Crown

This dull ache that pains my routine
Turns joyful red to green
And throws up a screen to smiling

Excessive incantations make witchdoctors
Of those who wish the cup of alchemic gold
They fold into despair or padded cells
Reason captive to something insubstantial
Saddling youth with problems of the old

This cholera of the imagination and slacking
Of the mind leave behind
The waves of the inner life's sea
Churning babbling endlessly

Routine in its teens a growing adolescent terror
A wearer of a grim grin of vacuous irony
It devours my gifts
Leaving desires of unrealized hopes

The limbo must end
The change begins
The vibrant flutter of light
Light growing softly in the soul
Imagination and I becoming one
In a questing body
Usurping the oppression of repetitive triviality
To add the fiery ruby to Creation's crown.

A Noble Fry

Extreme dream masters having a go at moons
Loons too drugged to answer the call
Of waking Minos as the labyrinth walls echo
The bullish reprimand

Decked in purple
The princess pursues her mate
The diamond's ready
The groom's rather late
Delayed by Circe's grand design
He wallows like a swine in her palatial sty

As the ceremony lingers on
The groom has a ring in his nose
Preventing the smell of Circe's trap
Too enthralled by the Temptress's spell

The King's in check
The Queen's not well
The princess stands in purple waiting
The prince is too young for dating
And the groom's in sensual swoon
Out in the harbor the sailors cry "Ship ahoy!"
While high above, too far to see, menace looming
The groom wallows and grunts
One of Circe's favorite stunts

Midnight arrives
The Princess fast in hope
The hidden player emerges from night-clad slope
The groom can't break Circe's spell
Enthralled fully
He porks his way to Hell
A noble fry

Down comes the hidden player from the slope
Woos Sophia with many a Cabbalistic kiss
Places a diamond on her purple clad form
Both mount steed and quickly elope
Circe's old man arrives on the scene
Sees the groom in such an obscene light
Leaps from his boat with green handled knife
Cuts his swinish throat
Throws his head into the moat

Sophia rejoices
The hidden player removes his mask
Eros and she to the bridal chamber retire
Circe's thrown from her kingdom of heat
Yet outside the kingdom men can still
Hear her siren song full and sweet
Yet draw back for fear of mind and meat.

Offended Love

Bloodless vampires of generalized mind
Eros strangled by duty, syllogistic pride
In this vision sterile philosophers smile
Threatening punishment to those moved by
Slandered love
Too many hypocrites raise aloft the skeletal idea
To rule men and women of flesh and blood
With laws and commandments they begin
Some necessary for ordered life
Some necessary to limit strife
But when love is declared a sin
Or demoted to bloodless contemplation
All relations become ghostly.
When the root of Life is strangled at the source
At this even the gods are ashamed
By this civic apologetic some win fame
Kill God in dialectics
Put Eros in chains.

Into

Into her iris my soul leaped
Seized love
Deny it she will
Undeniable that surge of warmth
Her soul mated to mine

Though she's married
Observant ones find
Love manifests
Though legalities bind one's action
There'll be no retraction of spiritual truth
Into her iris my soul leaped
Seized love.

Triumph

Of my true future love in past tense I sing
Presuming it a certainty of destiny's ring

So long your presence haunted my dreams
So long your magic wove a spell around me
So long I saw not your face
Then like grace
You and I met
   Our eyes centered
   Our spirits met
We dared delve that love with sigh and sweat
Together we soared above the chaos
Now
After that moon-bright night
Now
After our souls took flight
   So much we see
   So much we understand
   Beyond paltry logic
   We take our stand
O Eros! Sands of time be strewn
Before our fated feet
Together we'll live though hatred
Dogs our heels
And at the altar of fierce trials we will kneel
No matter the cost
All of it's worth
What we feel and live.

Cupid's Eagle

O proud Eagle of Mind
What did you think you'd find
Entangled in Love's changeable vine
What distilled wine of particular pleasure
Would take measure of your encompassing soul

How bold you were in the beginning
Bubblingly happy and grinning
Your heart pulsing at the thought of winning
A beautiful treasure of womanhood
O what an imagined good!

Now it has led to disillusion and heartache
Dawn has found you in Melancholy's fold
Covered with a laurel wreath of despair
While your soul is rife with rebellion at
Having been captured with a sigh and a ruse
What you had to lose never occurred to you
You wanted only Beauty and Love
But got a treacherous sparrow disguised as a dove

Again O Eagle
With clipped wings you fly
To the mountain of healing solitude.

Beauty Wakes Me

Beauty wakes me deep
Rouse the soul from dream centered sleep
Pledge my eyes a jewel
A secret full and sweet
O woman of beauty
You delight the eye
Whether or no
Our bodies together lie
Keep your stateliness
For by and by
Stands a poet
With appreciative eye.

Subtle Psychism

A timeturn is a spacerun
Eyes amoeba out love rays
Galaxy spins
Irises issuing ecstasy
Inward touching thought
Dissolved vivid cinema in sleep
Weepers processional sadness
At loves lost
So needs fill the ether

Telepathic lovers roam the night dream waves
Astral travelers moving to the music of Eros
In the night men and women
Love at a distance
They meet by vested coincidence
Or expert design

All who know vow silence
Subtle eyes see all
Emanating love finds its mate
Dream driven fate defies reason
Revelation is hidden in code
The key is a matter of inner translation
The answer is relational coordination
Truth an erotic jest given a text
Provoke the snake from the sage's hair.

Muse Magic

My love is so beauteous
Her hair's so fair she's not seen
No color has she as far as I've seen
Yet her eyes are wonders and so serene
Call her Sophia if you will
Her aura if could be seen
As deep as the ocean's green

Her presence an angel's raptured embrace
And for such a prize
I hope you realize
I had to open my eyes
Transmute the base to gold's refine
Govern the body and higher being unwind
Magnetize my soul to her special kind
Crash the barrier of a new dimension
Struggle and fall before ascension

And as the silvered moon arose at night
She and I took flight as in a dream
She soothed my loneliness made me keen
And whenever I began to fall
Sounded from her spirit's great call
She's my love that's all.

Sleep Darling

Sleep my love
So dreams may bring me back
To you

While you dream on your bed of roses
I carry the sting of thorns in my soul
Dead is the former self I thought I knew
Free
Now I see you in a new way
Though love reigns over our kingdom
Morning brings the aurora of light
And as usual
We smile and say "Hello."

Snow Crystal Flakes and Geometric Ubiquity

Morning the rise of wonder
The fall of creation's veil…

All falling snow drops
Diamonds at Tiffany
Geometric crystal lattice work
Association of form and structure
Elegance beauty aptness
With imagined moods
A dreamy mind
Look!
The water drop
The pearly tear
The dress that all the women wear
Quality and poise to bear
Admiration
Her diamond there
A high class
Love affair.

Basics

Full moon obscured by clouds
The howl of dogs long and plaintive
Beaming sun scenes
Gulls gliding the ruffled lake
What people say and do
Lovers whispers
Elopers in haste
Visions of Gods
Shiva Vishnu Brahma Yahweh
And others
Fears and Loves
The strange unknown
The smile of a friend
Weather tantrums
Sun to rain and snow to shine
Holidays.

The Bed: Frontier of Invention

Dream on my love with eyes bright
As far off Andromeda...

Descartes wrote geometry in his bed
Babies a million conceived in a bed
A quota each day gets up out of bed
Drunkards surviving d.t.'s in their bed
Acts illegal committed in bed
With sheer delight
Lecher lives in his bed
Just like the chronic invalid

Courts produce evidence
It happened in bed
Comic a honeymoon
Awkward in bed
A lack of discretion
Get caught in the bed
Take you from bed
To graveyard
Dead.

Nova

There in the dark reaches of space far deep
Where our eyes cannot see
The swirling hurricane of a nova
Over a million years ago
Gave light to leathery-winged birds and stubby moss
And reached back far enough before
The first grunts of cave men gaping
When we could not see or be
There was first a star

Born burning
Fading farther in space-time
Extended continuum and light rushing
Over heaven's expanse
Ending on a poet's pupil of
Imagination
Giving quanta to the point of
A moving pen
Giving a
What when
To a
What has been
Giving a pinpoint of light to
Dark field
An image to the expanse before
The myth which echoes yet
"Let there be light...!"

The nova evolves deeper shadows and shades into
Brilliantine colors which the eye cannot see
Except imaginatively

Needs only a telescope a spectroscope
To register its spectrum spread
A determined look to see
Indeterminacy
Enter mortal pupils of a poet's imagination
Grinning on infinity with love and wonder.

Charades

Parade of poses in legion
The social games of insincerity

We're called mad who
Rebel against conformist sham
And offered drams of forgetfulness

There is no forgetting
The thievery and bloodletting
Official and not

The knot of Fate
Disallows
Libra to go unbalanced   .

Enter Mars and Venus his bride
Their children to be
Stellar wonders.

Past Time Games

The story's still the same
After the work day
Stumbling to find his way
To love
To fall face first
Into beery float top foam
Then left quite alone
To stagger late to home

Cold cold the city air
The cloud-dazed mind is lost
To love
Discourses to the wall
Falls heavy in debate
Hallucinating figures
Like fates
Haunting his abandon
Irritating low cast vision
He falls asleep kicking the cat
Then dreams of long lost peace

He's a moderately successful man
Double-chinned Romeo
Fifty-year-old sport
Every woman with youth in air
Recalls his stare
He's plagued with rheumatism
A wife at home
Just can't leave it alone

Games games high or low
Rich and old playing along
To misery

Lives with statistical calculation
Don't you weep laugh forget much for fear
Keep the social world awhirl
All on the dear Earth's face together
Eons apart
Between misery
Wry laughter
Smiles and tears
And years
So many years for man to grow
But to ease the mind
He chooses to be blind.

To Die Unfulfilled

To die unfulfilled
Is to live in fear
Ever watchful of the other's eye
A coward's life

To go from this world knowing one
Has never been fully oneself .
This is a life far too lacking in truth

A time spent in bowing for small praise
Unmanly haze of puppetry
Cowed by the crowd's hypnotic routine
Afraid to issue a dream into reality
Silly in fact to tears
Caught in the shears of opinion
Never claiming one's dominion
Of selfhood
Not living freely and true
Having allowed oneself to be shackled
To the cross of gossip nailed to fear
Limited by lack of love
Curiosity in chains
Dodging truth to please
Fellow prisoners in the same
Conspiracy of self-deception

To die unfulfilled
In the fear of sudden ecstasy
Meeting a strange woman's eyes
Stifle a smile to suit yesterday's mood
A barren life
Too limited to scream
Laugh aloud
Hidden in a shroud of monotone normality

Denying the total range of possibility
Denying the instincts in the soul's key vein
Letting habit encrust one to a dull refrain

Hesitation to leap at once into life's whirl
Living vibrant and full
To deny the inward urge
The vital surge
Is to suicide the self
In lifeblood fire
To die unfulfilled.

See See

See see the mind's great sea
Tears and laughter in symphony
Chicanery and honesty
All the world misery
And joy
Greeks did treachery to Troy
Celebrated in literary key
Oblivious to morality
Unsung mysteries degraded to insanity
In this negative cosmology

Sages left irrefutable testimony
To witness the soul's highest flight
From intuition to the astral light
Most today believe the skeptics right
Some leave their souls to hatred's bite

When genius in death bid goodbye
The mob (you see) will not cry
Their verdict is that dreamers
Aspire too high
Their own fates they do not defy
So higher spirits they deny
Beyond the utility of base souls
All that's noble late gains hold
Of the mind of man.

The Will to Live as an Intuition of Purpose

In the dream was said
"Tides of my love sweep the realm of life and all alive
Find my love and sympathy
Empathic I am all and all that will be
I was created to be successively transformed
Down the ages of eternal presence
In transformation of creative energies
All I find in me
A cosmic wholeness unaware in the particular of being
Part of one great love suffering being
I am the I and eye of all I's and eyes…"

Given the chance of being
A baby is aware of having a purpose

Into the world squeezed by labored thighs
He opens his eyes to survey the chaos
He'll organize into palpable patterns
Creative with every breath
The cells wear and repair
Destroyed
Replaced
Again and again in cycle repeat

Oedipus Sphinx riddle of man
Each entity lives in cycles
Drawn teleologically to his own
Realization gestalt
Each person senses some plan
Unfolds for self and others

In dispensing desires hopes and needs
Nature's democratic
She weighs the elite with talent to express
The range of her treasure in each one life

To think
It all begins with a flash of passion
And a victorious spermy seed.

Dialogues of Uncertainty: The Beginning of Wisdom

Into the Act Out of Magnetized Relations Alcoholic...

Set pride aside to search for the truth
Uncertain
But venturing into unexplored probables
Weighing variables other than stated clichés
Unleashing creative energies
In a healthy exchange of ideas
Open to the other's views
But assessing with suspended pride
Leaving pulling rank outlawed
No degree hiding either
Drink and talk on
For there's wisdom in weighing
Not irately inveighing
Even after the fourth martini
Or
Whatever.

The Sage Saint in a Militaristic World

Look at Methuselah's Face!

Spirit doctor
Harbinger of human hope
Mystery dweller called by
Some country to war
Images of union and peace
Dreamer of planetisation
Consummate appreciator of beauty
Master over self with yogic fidelity
Guardian of ancient wisdom
Mystic lover
Wonder seeker in nature's pulse
Lover of perfection and will
Seeker of the mystery of birth and death
Mission walker on the waves of time

Face uplifted in the falling rain
Einstein takes a walk
The Holy Grail exerts its spell
Pure hearted throes of longing:

> Like him
> Others too are forced to
> Sorrow.

Spirit Fusion

Out of confused strivings
Comes the adaptive
Center of realization
Invocation to conscious
Streams of expansion
Dreams revelations
Situational settlement
Of questions

Over the rainbow are mysteries
Yet to be decoded
Life must become sincere
And persons happily whole:

    Most fear the transition.

History Lesson

For all would-be Caesars to know
Time flows on and empires surely fall
The blood of transformation cannot be stopped
By force and fraud
Nature rights all excesses in the cyclic

Permanency is but an illusion foisted on matter
Change is Nature's law
That which is fluid will triumph
Over social fossilization
Nature cannot be arrested with blind force
It will erode all obtuse effort
It will burst all bricked fortifications
It will yield only to the genius of fluidity

What good were Hitler's mighty legions of war?
They too came to pass
Those who would survive
Learn from the wise fish:
Swim
And bite no hooks of illusion.

Love General

He commanded an army of lovers
All under orders to save Nature's
Great work
Leapers in time
Space hoppers
His stars he wore in his brain
His Pentagon
The galaxy's center.

Lone Wolf

He stays to himself
And thus misunderstood
Carrying on his creative work
Too much socializing kills the creative spirit
Too little leads to barren hack work
Solitude's my quirk
Speaking without haughtiness or smirk
An artist needs solitude to issue creation
Devastation of privacy is a major vice
And advice out of ignorance is a nuisance

The Lone Wolf follows a star
While most others follow the pack
And neon lights.

Spells

You will fall under the spell of seasons
Shed your pains and feel the change
Become a new you

You've come from shed I's that are old
Let each day embrace you unified
Observe children and re-learn to be
Curious eager and free

Let yourself go into new regions of knowing
There is no end of new being
Your self is as infinite as the stars
Let yourself wander beyond walls
Steadfastly stand tall
There are new lands waiting for you
And new people waiting to go with you
Turn the leaf of your routine page
This is the Aquarian Age.

Language

Let something be said
From slang to twang
Meant in many ways
With associations streaming
The elusive vocalization of meanings
All screening what's never totally revealed
Now inflicting wounds to the ego's shield
Later soothing apologetically to heal

Language the great plastic rhythm
The great reality label field
Makes it possible for us to say
So many things
In a pause or phrase
Putting others to sleep
Waking them from a daze.

Reason's Bad Season

Reason on a treasonous trolley
Running wild
Assaulting the heart all the while
Statistically assessing a child's smile
While grave old men chew gum out of boredom
Reason too can surrender to
Whoredom of the spirit

Infinitude's immortals laugh
At the equational imposture
And their laughter echoes in the
Gurgling baby smelling a flower
Or a genius in rapture over a trifle

The stern statisticians frown over
Their figures and graphs
Tire at last
They too surrender to novelty
In sleep
Their dreams lacking reason or rhyme
But in the morning they resume
Their trolley ride with a single mind
While Nature plays a game in double time
With uncatalogued rhyme.

Surging Forth

Happy surging forth!
Naked truth
Source golden secret
The inner dwelling of the King
It speaks in dulcet tones

The suitors heated delight
Touched by budding life come to fruition
After winter's gestation of loving thought
Bee and bird in wing-spread flight
An aeronautic diminutive sight
Two lovers concealed in moon clear night
Two microcosms in passion's light

The alchemist searches for the stone
Janus' two faces have shown
That double vision stands alone

The Milky Way
Iris of the sky
Spins as Greenwich mines it earthbound time
Timeless themes realized in symbic dream
The eyes are clear the conscience clean

A mother-to-be in labor begins to cry
O youth! You too must come here
Screaming with sharp inrush of air
Living to hurt love enjoy and cry
And foolish old men set the impossible seal
That the Real is higher than the Ideal
All must decide as we together reel
In life's great dance:
    Most find heaven in finance.

Prayer to Earth

O solitary soul
Stained by the actual terrors of earth
Encircled by ignorance and vulgarity
What is left for you
But vertical ascent into wisdom and love
When inspiration showers you
Sing to posterity

Though your friends know you not
From your suffering make a knot of will
Appeal to phantoms rather than deaf ears
Let every attack on you redouble your strength
Every doubt quicken your resolve
If alone you must be
Fly into the arms of contemplation
Keep your value in secrecy
Let silence crown your dignity
Flee from profanity like a plague
Joy in the mind
Find all your treasure within
The world is jealous of value
Shake the hand of no spiritual vulture
It leers for your death.

The Power of Eros

Great mover of life on Earth
Vestal virgins at the hearth
Satyrs frolicking with sensual mirth
Your dominion extends across the ages
You've ruled fools and sages
Imprisoned men you've led to ruin
Others you've led to a burial urn
Joy promised issued woe
Wild oats your denizens sow
When up shines the romantic moon
Dark places yield sigh and cry
Sufferings you've watched
From the heights of power
As your will has drugged poets to tell
Of your great sway over man and beast
Or of beasts seeming men
As testimony to you
A Grecian funeral was prelude to a feast
Never sated you never rest
Counter to convention we find
Casanova at his best under a woman's dress
Lived in danger for your name
Though reviled he inherited fame
For all living things know this truth
Your favorites are the bold and youth.

Soft Elegance

Fine velvet
Rubies
Sweet wine
Dinner for two
Grecian decor
Encore of candlelight
Paintings by Raphael
Air of strings
Clean colorful bed
Goodnight my love.

Mirrored Revelation

Slip of the tongue
Fast flew the withheld thought
Experience taught by error
And discovery a certainty
She was guilty but
Pride locked her vanity
Profane thoughts in the neighborhood church
Prying out secrets
Talking too much

One day she confessed to her full-length mirror
It cracked into pieces with loud report
She swore like a sailor
Kicked the cat
Powdered her face
Put on her favorite hat.

Caverns

Falling courage
lost into darks of the mind
ghosts ghouls gargoyle chills
shot through forbidden revelry
the censor sleeps on its own inertia
sympathetic thoughts spill up
the conscious spout
then the demons come out
screaming for a hearing
demanding equal time with the straight and narrow
advocates of the curving and wide
seeming quite annoyed at having to hide
to please the despot conventional morality
threatening revolution
mass dreams invasions
division in the ranks
slips of tongue
jitters of the nerves
fearful nights
tight muscles
headaches
dyspepsia
general tremens of the confidence
and an all-out state of libidinal smog
cast on the flimsy film of lucidity
no compromise available
the inner surge leads only to variation
growth against the sluggish will
tied to the wheel of habit
tilling a barren field of doing as others
do
resisting the feel to yield
and be utterly
Unique.

Brain Chain Miracle

Elements eternal
The world's great panorama
Images in the sensitive brain
Marvelous organ of receptivity
Contemplating smooth-skinned nudes
This life pulsing electricity
Chemicated to human revelry
Living thoughts
Falling waters
Pain and slanting slides of moonbeams
All feeling
Organic awareness
Death refusing and cosmic musing
The lifting of feet to the rhythm of the
Rushing sea
Breakers on the shores of memory
Sand wet with water receding
Voice given excitement
At power driven climax
Man in woman
Desire cascading in a music of murmurs
Grimacing faces in ecstasy

Epic action dreaming
Executed with ballet beauty
Occurring with energic pride
Starry universe mirrored within-without
In and out the signals run
Activate
Integrate
And
Ponder the question of Fate.

Perceptics

Leapfrog dimensions
Infinite planes in action
Sweeps of fancy
Blocks and boxes
Plains and planes
Differences

Too much
Silence
Before the symphony

Grades of release from
Boring TV'd episodes
Pains of a vulgarian's antics
Ocean sounds
Spiritual groundswells
Dreams of multi-heavens
Hidden treasure in musical measure
Cycle invariants of love affairs
Beams of wonder from children
When he's near
X8 images and all that can't be described
Infinities of what ifs.

Pause in Thought

A fallen flower felled
By an enthusiastic dog
In spring heat
Mimic of man
Ununderstood relations
Implicit designs
Actions interpretable
Reflection of mental perplexities
Into concrete examples of
Weather like rain
Countless scenes
All spring is blossoming and green.

Gemnal Dream

Dreams of rubies red
And agate layered onyx
Gemnal splendor
And diamonds spread
Before emerald sheen
The keen green of jade
Around
A mound of feldspar
Opaline wonder with cultured pearl
All wonder in a dreamy world.

Lyric Figures

Ever moving rhythm
Muralistic marvelous music
Seen shimmering in love's fire dance
Of August noon heat
With hubbubing grottos of fantasies
Stampeding images of grass
Greening with imagination's weaving
Of tapesterial forms
Figmenting the clear acceleration of exhilaration
Spinning madly widely
Wisely ranging far from sleep

Intrusion of waking dreams
Circe's stream of piggish invitations
Making faces at the Graces
While they're gossamer dancing with smiles
Into the weeping wailing wind

Songs calling harpers in processional fancies
All moons beaming a range through ever present time
Turning the Universe on a complexity pulse
Wrapping life in unity
Yawning Caprice sees it all
Going on process wholeness streaming

Dreaming in waking sleep
Taking stock and shock at past dreams
Waking to Beauty's clarion clear ring
Azure sky thunders and it rains while
Plunderers of the treasure
Measure matter degraded to baseness
Discovery rolling ruses of disguises
Figuring full secrecy of mimicry
When the proper tale is told
Stern command shouted baldly and bold
Unfold!

Sea Scenes

Fresh the surging sea
Rich salty seaweed
Ocean-creatured smells
Ships pulling in putting out to sea
Moby Dick musings
The Captain's yell
"Full speed ahead"
Echoing memories
Sea gulls chatter
Harboring expectations
With their whited forms
Spume ambrosia searching
Hurricane figures
Water fugues
China seas
Breeze from the East
Chinamen with queues trembling wet
Crouching low in boats riding the waves
Gliding riding with troughing waves
Rushing over top of the sea-y deep
Davy Jones' locker broken open
In a raging storm
The pirate's glass eye given a cleaning
After days at sea
Wailing winds
All's green
The First Mate weeps
Man overboard!
The Navy's fleet of lonely men
A lighthouse's broken glass
Hanged high
Hells jerking
Beautiful man
Innocent dear Billy Budd

Captain Hook out of Disneyland spins dizzy
With ticking clock the gator stalks
Dangers lurk the boom halyards
Monsters sweep the pressured deep
A giant squid hid in sunken treasure ship
Slips with suckers ready for seeking sailors
So the sea may as well the ocean be
Water transcending the name
Scenes flashed on the mind's eye
Framed projections in the brain.

Diamonds

Crystal fusion prismatic light broken
Color spread majestic patterns
Geometrix shining heavenal stone
Connoting far lands
Marriagal symbol
Acts of love
Losing value as icon of unslaked greed
Exclusive lust of a pack of thieves
Resting form irregular
Then cut to imagination's need
The heart's delight
Of carbon worn in the glittering sun
Shown with a star-led smile
While beauty exclusive of moralic fashions
Exudes its care over
The gem the wearer will wear
A matter of vanity.

Atlas

The heavy headed Atlas shrugged and let the world
Fall to the outward orbit of space
Then took a rest
Hoping that when it stopped falling
He, Atlas
Would be a god

And yet he trembles at the thought
A noble act or just aching muscles
Made him loose the world
Whether his spirit lagged
Or the pain of labor pried his fingers loose
Or did sleep overcome his resolution?

He watches the earth fall yet
He
Was too much to dwell within it:
                    His shadow the night
                    His eyes
                    The sun and moon
Now
He's just a tired myth
Occasionally
A sculptured Titan.

Sonics

Here comes the sonic boom
Rash of crash of blue window glass
Stained church windows splinter to pagan
Disorganization
Vibration registration on the sensitive skin
Red rashes of clashes on grating nerves
A gentleman's momentary loss of verve
A swerve of car over the railing
Caught by shock
The surprise chaosing eye and hand
Mellow pulling along of an Amish wagon
The mounting ranting of angered citizenry
Over the trembling ceiling goes roar
The deaf mute thinks the day's a bore.

Historamus

Sometimes I cry
As history bleeds misery down the ages
The savage mobs
Those unregarded sages
Throbs of intense conflict

Bodies strewn on the pyres of idolatry
Why so much suffered pain?
Nature continues her stern play
Day by day the dramas unfold
Conflict and conflict untold

No good to scorn the universe
We hear only our futile echoes
Or worse yet prayer echoing to infinity
Without answer
If there's a divinity
It's cryptic

Clot by clot human blood still drops
Prometheus yet chained to the vulture-tended rock

Lately some philosophers say all is an absurd joke
We choke on their nadiric revelation
Cling to pleasures and treasures of illusion

Out of this confusion
Must come swift with no illusion
Like sunburst to a cloudy day
A master of reality and ironic play.

Volatile Silence

Out of volatile silence comes meaning
And it is a symbol beneath words and above gesture

Consider the weather, madness, and Man
The span of chaos when most fritter away time by killing it
Protesting that fast time kills all that temporarily lives

To break the pessimistic gloom we swing to wild distraction
Blaming it all on an inclination an inspiration for
Laughter

Aware of being a neophyte to master maiden learning
A fool of the great modern world
Mind absorbed in other's thought
Bewailing my own expressed indirectly
Some think me profound yet
Bacon overshadows my attempt at eloquence

I am aware of my sleep
And salute fellow dreamers in
Our mutual charades of realization

The effort is silent
Yet the effect erotically explosive
If you read me
Live the lines and sleep between them.

Rose Rose

Rose Rose bid the singers free time to sleep
Over wakeful studies found in brook and creek
Plant herb rock and star
Who can ban the mind of man from afar?
Who can put the wisdom of love in the spar of a Grecian ship?
Who can seal the lie from sweet Helen's lip?
And trip the alarm the jester will do
If only he's rid himself of smirkful pride
Bury his query find fast answer
Hard it is to quench thirst with vinegar
Yet the smell of sulphur is incentive to a mask
Take to task the rebellious butterfly and cry "False smile"
Awhile the drama will continue to play
While Master Greybeard herds his sheep
Only the cliffs are steep
Yet Pluto dogs his coolness
Athene too gives her gracious assent
Platonic veils of mysteries are rent
After the king's great raged face inflames the pawns
The king and queen retire to marital bed

Where Eros is liberally fed
Beyond Sophia's diadem reign the Philosophi
While demagogues shout in the name of Vox Populi
Give the jester some poppy and let him sing
His jokes will entertain as well as sting
A cosmic tatterdemalion with lyric fling
Dances his dance with abandoned leap
Rose Rose bid him sleep
Sleepwalker he is:
   His dream's too deep.

Iris

All seeing eye
Swirl of galaxy
Pattern for mutated magician
Centering of force in third eye
All seeing but not seen
Surveying the scene
of earthly things
Longing for space and heaven.

Gradation

The beginning is a test of intent
The ascent is an act of faith
Step by step occultation occurs
Incursion of instruction
At every mistake
This the rigid rule of initiation
The mysteries are all around in
Blood, tree and flower
At the summit
All seems providence.

Bio-Mathic Reflections

A square is the four major races in figure
A triangle is partialistic alliance
A line is bigotry's limitation
A dot is individual egoism
A circle is humanity's wholeness
But a sphere is the Earth in fullness
And all mathematic figures glyphs
Of the human mind and body social
And more complexity awaits the explorer
The deplorer is non-mathematic or literal

No good comes from assumed superiority guttural
Or pigmented vanity
Leave the ape his cave
Deprive the savage his enclaves of exclusiveness

Culture's diverse concentric
Civilization's a rigid whore of iron ore and gore

Give to circled man his dominion
Criticize opinion and make the eagle pinioned
Face left as the spiral tensions grow
Perfect the durable hypothesis
Extract the essential patterns architectural
And melody a tune of geometric beauty

Many will die for a truth
Little figurine of bias it may be
But let truth make us live
Knowledge make us free
Become yourself
My equation's computed
Don't copy me.

Power Circle

An evolving human being of energy
Reaching for the divine
Circling in a place of occultation
Around that mystic circle in force
The Aethen guide pursues the shaping
With angelic wisdom
Draping a being to unknown design
Molding his body
Disciplining it to an unknown task
Drawn to the moon
Cosmic surge!
Mind enveloped by fateful stars!
Finding the copula of creation in constellations
Energies in rain water
Drawing this force to inner being
Willing
Trying
Willing life and more life

Beyond the surface strife
In deep harmony
All pettiness becomes fertilizer
For a strong tree
Deep rooted yet branching heavenward
Sky pulls while roots reach deep into stable earth
Living love in sap-like currents flow
Yet soar the plane of reason
Intuit the astral sphere
Infusion of grace into a questing soul
Bold the central explorer's will

Out of invisibility spills
The power of direction
Onto the world's wheel
Shaping a man to the world's will.

Einstein

A genius is an artist of Life. He will make something of anything.
—*Anonymous*

Gushed
White sainted hair
Rising
Like your creation personified
Though your gentle face and electric hair
Express the innocence of the saint
The form of the artist
Your wisdom applied became a flower of evil
A toadstool
It became a mushroom burning human flesh
And Hell incarnate in Hiroshima troubled your soul
You grew weary of man and his warlike ways
His barbarisms and unkind feelings

You lived for truth
And died searching for unity in all nature
What love must have lived in your very existence
What far and wide terrain did you turn to
Watching the stars within and without
What divine intimations must have given meaning to all your life
Your children brought you pain
Yet you searched and searched
And all who see you on a poster
Or beaming from a book
Know that man has far to go
Before he'll ever understand
What you found in alien regions
And airy lands
Waked from your dreams
Exploding the heavens
With energy's scream
Brought down to earth.

Lore

Eager with new knowledge he began to talk
Began to speculate with incautious abandon
Much to his unwise mind's dismay
His mystic brothers turned to say
Quiet be
Things of the spirit are not for the profane
Examine reason the answer's clear
Talkers in the past have paid dear
Let them feed on the shells and husks of
Ancient wisdom filtered through the ages
Sages keep their lips sealed
Let the profane think the arcane unreal.

Energics

The trees grew stronger root to leaf
The talk got meaning
Became brief
Bodies hardened
Truth replaced erroneous belief
Intelligence soared
In a general way
Eye to eye became communications way
Error and hypocrisy had had its day
The greatest humans did serenely say
"Move higher and higher or get out of the way"
The doctor did his job for reasonable pay
The farmer stopped cheating his horse of hay
Earth launched its first starship beyond the Milky Way.

Elixir

O that stone
Philosopher
Pressed in the alembic of love
Forged in the crucible of suffering
Mercuriated by knowledge
Silvered by opposition
Gold squeezed from creative tension
Ascension into Beauty's kingdom
Rayed through and through by Akasha
Beyond common cognition
Hidden in the cloud
That surrounds the hidden crown
From the heights
Divine fire brought down

With an ecstatic shudder
Earth abounds with the holy mantra.

The Key to Anti-Gravity is the Creative Mind

Low low swing the saucery machine…

Abandon the bullet!
Cry not for the missiles on scrap heaps
There are better things!
Study the flying saucer
To find an economic design
With aeronautic beauty
And speedy climb
Clarify its propulsion system
And learn to imitate
A natural form of flight
At the height of speculation
Seize the secret that makes it go
It may be that it runs
On controlled electromagnetic flow
Or coherent sonar pulses
May speed it so
Anyway it's a craft can be flown with
A jovial disposition
And 90 degree precision change of position.

Sun Centers and Galactic Imagination

Pick a star
It may be your soul's
If so you'll enter history
Fascinating and brilliant…

Other star systems
Other forms
Other minds elsewheres
All this man must
Prepare to meet
…Skeptical whispering in the cosmos
From a dust-mote Earth
Radio waves from Quasar X
What utters the static reaching
Earth's mechanical ears?

Suns in millions
Starry oceans
Blue suns
Red suns
Pink suns
And life
Waiting
For Earth to grow.

The Last Cosmocraft

The last cosmocraft is leaving soon
That high noon of preparation
Then into the stellar night
A mind flight

The mysterious traveler
Disappears from sight
On Earth he protected
Angel flight.

Psi Cosmos Religion

No churches
The sun the moon the stars
The deep volumes of space
Rushing rays of light
Thought diffusing it all
God a cybernetician
Steersman of worlds
Control of planetary dynamics
Architector of living forms
Day determiner
Life infuser
Reincarnater supreme
Synthefluxer of dreams.

Psi Master

He knows the mind
Moods all kind and Greek mystery
Esoteric lore
The stars in course
He fathomed the Sphinx and Revelations
His labor penetrated the cosmos
Encased in a small body of clay
He sped to light and
Wisdom rocked him in arms
Like a tender mother her son
He changed with the galaxy
And no one knew
He was in all them and they saw
Only what light
Their eyes
Could bear.

Grand Architect Eternal

Span the universe with signal and sign
Pattern and sigil and esoteric design
Life infused with structured precision
The carpenter's plane and mathematician's rule
Learning students in nature's great school
Bud of tree and cathedral stone
Rosicrucian mystery and Freemason lore
The store of humanity's treasure
All governed by rule and measure

Great energizer of all action
Light's refraction and its laws
Effects mated to cause
Outpouring of creative sight
Spinning galaxies and nebular might
Microcosmos in selfsame plan
The Universe's design inscribed in Man.

Foetal Dreams and Infinite Memories

Ever floating watery world
Amnioticular sac
An involution of starry worlds
Rushing dreams of electrons
Coming going with patterns of nebulae
Structuring a growing brain
All creation given again in minima
Of maxima evolution of the cosmos
Star points color sun spreads in
An expanding mind
Watery vibrations from Neptune's spin
With ominous Pluto circling
An omen of hellish premonition
The planet nine
The month to be aborn the Earth
Memories long of lives before lived
All short of perfection
Dawning again to familiar circumstance
To face the compass four
Awakening from dreams of infinite rule
Dimensions of mind obscured
In the transit of birth into a terror world
Of minds bound to vain vagaries of body
Muttering curses at the world
Forgotten stars
The foetal kick and float
Against the mother's womb
She thinking in terms of limit
The foetus limitless in mind over space
Leaping light years to mighty Orion
Dipping in the Dipper for soul-rich milk
Mystic ilk of moods
Serene wisdom
Vast flights of feeling the mother little divines
Of her growing creation

Soon waking from dreams with knowledge obscured
Slapped roundly on the bottom
The indignity
To breathe.

Interval

The interval is all pulse time
Pulse repetition
Beyond the light is the source
Beyond that pulse racing thought
Fraught phrases and phases shadow

Waving out to sea
The tides carry fish unaware of their watery medium
So deep
Thus are men unaware to air they breathe
Comes the wind blowing and surging the ocean of air
All one of a piece
Nature's great cosmic ocean
Bearing all on its crest
Processing evolution's test.

Treasonous Reason

Bare reason itself leaves one cold
Bold must be the seeker of truth
The heart too has its wisdom
No argument can stop realization
Love too has its mysteries
Not to mention unfathomable deity
Proudly logicians have sway where laziness reigns
Reason is a lazy obedient dog
And lies of life again and again
Sophistry's its lucrative twin

Love has arcanas of wonder
And how many lost in love have use for syllogisms
Recall the mother rescuing her child
Though danger surrounds like a venomous aura
All that's true cannot be said
The body and spirit has too much wisdom
To be limited to the head
Abstractions are an intellectual amusement
But creative life is power

Though the dialectician has his hour
Eros tramples over his superfluity
Ruling rebellious life through eternity.

The Only Way

The only way to stay with man
After knowledge has dawned
Is to submit to some species of error

Man fears truth like some foul disease
Illusion and error put man at ease
Instead of love man settles for sexual tease
Instead of truth man settles for syllogistic flair
Instead of honest baldness
He settles for false hair
How can one deal with such an intractable creature
Who falsifies the past and murders the future.

O Beautiful Spring

O beautiful spring
You make my heart sing
Bringing love and vital things
Again and again
I thank the stars
For all the splendid hours of love
And sing praises to the moon
Not enough phrases for such wonders.

Stress View

Microbes and space probes
The Bishop's robe
LSD and strobe
Deranged man
In the circumfluent tow
Teeming millions on the globe
All hungry for life
Without malice propense
Yet at some expense
Problems detailed and immense
To this the oversensitive wince
Between the extremes fluctuate men of
Sense
All the world worried and tense
And the weak fold themselves in a dream
Poverty of thought
Manifold evasion
Hence
The only hope of world unity
Is outer space invasion.

Love Vertigo

Love vertigo
Lost in the beloved
Crystalline admiration
Full fated love
What beauty of form
What brightness of mind
So frightened at my
Total love
Leaving thinking of me
With love and fear
So near we were
Cherishing the moment we
Strayed into the province of God.

Dove Dance

The general's left tire went out in
Front of "Pleasant Skin" nudist colony
He stopped for a spare and found
Naked Truth
Strength left his resolve and he had
To relinquish his brass for all who passed
Soon he too was in the nude
And like a general surveyed the feminine field
But momentarily strategy failed
An erection and a willing blond initiated him
Into Sun Culture
On his way out he forgot his four stars
And hobbled on a flat to the nearest gas station.

The Leaf Falls in Fall to Complete a Cycle

Harmonic regular periods
Nature's heartbeat controls events:
>   the flow of blood
>   the rushing tides
>   weather variations

Cycles turn on themselves all around
The chill of fall
The acorn falls

Squirrels gather up nut by nut
As winter's wood gets cut
Pregnant mothers brace themselves
For the changing season

Bears hibernate
Curled head between feet

Snow greets northern factory workers
Treading to work

After all effort to save
The money goes to pay groceries and heat
In a cold icicly winter

The leaf falls in fall to lie
Dormant all winter long

In spring
Trees are green again
With circulating sap
While under a full moon
Lovers out on a lark
Carve names
In moon-illumined bark.

Olga

When Juliette cried and Helen of Troy stood fair
The time changing in colors spun
You have won the hearts of many men and
One comes with a vision spread over ages coming
Epochs gone
The Slavic ascendency and decline of empires
Your eyes the essence of burning wonder
Woman soft flesh
All beauty the strong vivid features of heraldry
Your walk giving joy to songs sung
By an observant lover

To kiss you a bliss far perhaps from
Actualization
Yet the lyric a praise to the love
Which seeks union in individuality with you

Embody forth the East in sensual
Fullness

Sureness yet all serene soul
Royal
A prince has come to mirror your quality
Like an unjealous Othello sane to life's demand
Electric would be our two's touch of hand
To understand the secrets of the eye
Quality and love all to mutual intelligence
Bringing souls found each other at last
Together

Find you this vision
Far from understandable
Yet the singer sees Olga
Laying Venus to cold statuette
And with full-blooded Woman-Goddess

Become flesh
Only the Poet of Life
Can bear approach without diminishment
Before Woman too strong
For weakling men pretending
To mature understanding

The Flying Dutchman of the Atomic Age
The Unknown Sage
The Man from Elsewhere sings love to
Olga

Years of loneliness seeking universal beauty
In particular woman
O
Your dark bright Greecic eyes
Windows to your soul
The vibrations ring in harmony

Aloof
Superior to the common strain
You hint of ultra-humane
The stages of evolved wonder
Of the human soul

So much love bound within your being
That even with eyes closed
The man of quality feels all the love rays
Envelop him in an ecstasy and
Flesh is alive with earthly love
And heavenly revelry

What rainbow could spread the spectrum
Colors of your mystery?
What mythic consciousness could issue forth
You in a Lilliputian world of
Half-men and half-women?

Whatever you are Olga you are whole
Destroying all reserve from your observant lover
Vanity may spur man to boast virtues
Built of idle dreams
Your lover is real and true
Love apologizes to none
But runs the risk of Fate
You were reincarnated to this hour
My gift to you in the orchid flower of love
While apart we remain
Your love and praise I'll ever sing.

The Honeybee (for myself)

Culture's pollen with empathy's nectar
For honey and the hive's perfection
A life along the creative vector
Sweetness and light in a useful confection

The inner voice comes to me

> You follow an ancient law
> Diverse ancestors saw
> You have to follow the age old will
> Work, create, fulfill
> And gather to live
>
> Suffer your wingful journeys over
> Brambles and anthills
> Finding fragrant flowers
> Not knowing exactly what you do
> It's built into you
>
> With sun dance and beauty calling
> You go to bring pollen and nectar dew
> Back to hivey hexagon
> This after lure of sweet invitancy
> Tending center petals to feed the hive
> Each day awaiting the sun to arrive
>
> Why for flowers do your wings
> Brave gusts, dust, for your work to
> Begin?
>
> Honeybee
> You're only free
> Chasing beauty and love with
> Duty's dominancy.

On stage at Greystone Hall, Kate Tucker hands Walter Delbridge the poems he's chosen to read. *Photo by Maya Miller.*

Delbridge is the guest of honor at the annual Art of Recovery gala at Greystone Hall in Akron. *Photo by Maya Miller.*

Tucker adjusts Delbridge's microphone. *Photo by Maya Miller.*

Backstage before Delbridge's performance. *Photo by Miriam Bennett.*

Once a Schizophrenic, Twice a Poet

Coordinates

Her lies created chaos enough
For ten blocks east
Latitude confusion
West longitude
Gracious father
Absolve these doubts
Let the sparrows fly south
For hors d'oeuvres sent singing the bill on credit
Happy go lucky
Cheesy luscious leg lifting
Stop
The top spins
Black negligee benedictions
My god!

Day Job

Monday names the high full moon
Sunday royal Heaven's patron of fire,
In between myths are legends
Dreams longing for life:
More than a five-day week or
Nine-to-five grind.

Clockwork

We put the hands of a clock
In our minds to define
The flow of time
Like a toothpick
In a hurricane:
The clock ticks
Time flows on …

Disintegration

To the last the clown does weep...
Steep is the plunge from the joyful pose.

Who's on First

The Devil gave God a reputation and ever since then
There's been hell on earth...

Father Forgive

O the mind its mysteries and visions deep
The confused parade of unleashed desires—myriad lusts
The cringing saint present in all—in the life of everyman
Genius, madman, beggarman, pipe-fitter and those who know
Not consciously what they do...

He Who Has Ears

People kill the truth
With a community of smiles
Intent on deafness...

In My Hermitage

In my hermitage I think not brood
What good to brood over life full of surprises
Best to enjoy Fate and fulfilled destiny

Think of the enchantment of making adults
Listen to children on a playground
Or the revolution of making people feel
What they actually feel
Instead of what they think they should feel

While I'm in solitude
There are young minds
Sometimes in old bodies
Questioning and questioning for new ways to live

In my hermitage I listen to music, I read books
And live a full life with myself
My true joys cannot be condensed to a small quotation
My anguish cannot be compressed into a mere complaint

Life is too full for too ready judgment and
Complaining is a sin against Fate

After music and books I relax
Party
Drink
Make love
A walk in the park
I go out
Then return to my hermitage.

I Kissed a Leaf Tonight

On a walk in rainy night
Spring trees full
Heavy leaf-laden
Ruffled by the capricious wind
The whole of Nature choired to my step
And Beauty leaped in sympathy
To my hungry soul looking deep
Into the tree's soul
Feeling roots cling to soil
Of earth
Breathing through its leaves
The tight protective bark
Its tough contoured limbs
Stretching
Branches reaching out
To moon and sun

Rain into it falling
Driven by the wind
Into a low-swung leafy branch
I walked in love with Life
I kissed a leaf and then walked on
So joyous and strong I came to be
That one might say
The tree was me.

Braintechtonics

The firing of new populations of neurons in the brain will bring greater areas of intelligence awake in a man. It is after extreme concentration and willing, do men of latent genius suddenly get a flash of illumination which illustrates this process. For this reason, many have erroneously felt it was knowledge coming from outside themselves. It would seem that way to men unaware of the immense potentials of the brain, which in most lie unused because not enough effort is made to trigger these unused neuronal nets.

The clinging to subjective and mystical ideas of one's gifts inhibits the *clear* working of these potentials which are indigenous to the brain's structure. These powers follow an isomorphic law. If little effort and perceptual engagement is made, then a man's brain will give him mediocre results. He will be plagued with conventional interests leaving most of his brain unused. If the effort and perceptual engagement is rich and intense, looking into the world and self, then the brain rewards one with Genius.

The formula $G=pi^2$ parallels for the mind what Einstein's $E=mc^2$ does for matter and energy. The brain and intelligence follow the same structural principles of the physical Universe. The formula is G(enius)=(equals) p(erceptions) times the mental constant i(magination)^2 (squared). This parallelization means that light and imagination are constants for matter and mind respectively. It also implies that matter and perceptions stored in the brain parallel each other. It leads logically for us to see that the translation of matter to E(nergy) releases enormous energy, just as translating perceptions and imagination into thought releases enormous psychic energy G(enius).

Why I Cry

I cry for the fools
who hear no music
I cry for the ears
who refuse the beat of life
I cry for the fools
who cannot see love in her face
I cry for the fools
who know not their own solitude
I cry for me
who sees the whole thing
I cry because it clears my eyes
so I may see, besides
there's an onion in the room.

Peculiarity

He was very peculiar
That
His distinction

Bone in the nose
Spikes on his dancing shoes
A wolfman's hand glove

He was such a rarity
That one day while he was away
Someone put a "For Sale" sign
On his door

Strange:
He bought it.

The Giant

When a man stands strong tall and free like a tree
the bushes whisper

When his branches reach out for sun and air
the shrubs fold in despair

When his roots reach deep for stability and nourishment
the bushes cling to the surface

When he sways and laughs with the winds
the bushes keep a straight and ugly face

Utility

Pandora's box hotter than the one Edison got on the ear
Barbs of hatred sharper than a savage's spear
Loosed rumors around a genius in isolation
Conducive to the rabble's craving of sensation
Far from the truth wander marketplace hawkers
Far from restraint are the stalkers of night
If man dare express his silent happiness
To him the hemlock of disregard
Falls hard on the shards of contempt and neglect
From the mob no higher nature exempt
Subject to swinish laughter ridiculous look
Instead of creating he's expected to cook
Utility is the measure of man's value today
One in many will disagree
He's shown to the madhouse to his neighbor's glee
Fastened in lies the world is snared
Escape to contemplation
And let them dissent
"Anti-social" and "ill-intent."
Such is the *paranoia* of cherished normality
They burned Bruno at the stake with vengeful formality

They lie in wait for their betters
To more quickly bind them in fetters.

Conformity Perspective

Dead laws
Dead customs
Spiritually dead people
They lust to rule and persecute
Those who follow a different star

This cruelty will end
Enlightened spiritual giants guard
The castle with the penetrating rays
Of light-emblazoned Justice
Soon the Angels' patience will end
So Beauty and Wisdom will come again

Conformity will assume its proper place
Merely a social cohesive for limited space
The strong will grow pace by pace
Weaving new patterns on Nature's face
The advent of a new race

Bold explorers of finitude facing infinitude's great expanse
Intuition pointed as a lance
Adverse to useless error
Calming the terrors
Of weakened minds
Architecting the future
For the conforming kind
Racing
The energy comes from Creation's root
New men keen of vision
Sure of foot.

Understanding Positive Mutations (Speculative Article)

Throughout history there have been positive mutations, that is, human beings who have crashed through the evolutionary barriers to new heights and the beginning of that which goes beyond ordinary man. There was DaVinci, cold as a Martian in his analyzing—observing, penetrating man, deciphering Nature and incorporating the world to his understanding. At his height, normal man's behavior must have struck him as that of apes or other lower species. For from such a vantage point normal human things are patently obvious and easily understood though disapproved of. All the conventional satisfactions of normal human beings could never fully satisfy a positive mutation.

To the positive mutation the Earth is just a starting point, not an end in itself. So-called normal life lacks the balance, reason, intelligence, coordination, wholeness and breadth of vision ingrained in the very transcendent nature of a positive mutation. He may as well *be* a Martian as far as others are concerned. It is usual for one such as this to be misunderstood because to the "average" man he is strange, a freak, or doesn't fit preconceived prejudices. In today's modern world there are exceptions. After all, now we have psychologists and psychiatrists who can help such Beings.

Another most famous positive mutation whose life has been distorted by churches, ignorant religious fools, and average people is He Jesus the Christ. The positive mutation Jesus Christ commanded a wisdom and control over forces which science is only beginning to seriously investigate and with a skeptical attitude at that. Christ was physically and genetically a positive mutant, but also spiritually the Son of that Unfathomable we call God. Science cannot understand Him because of its lack of spirit and religious devotion to augment its immense phenomenal knowledge.

The twentieth post-atom-bomb century is being invaded by an increasing number of +mutants who are deeply dissatisfied with the world's situation and man's behavior. Things are, after all, tinged with a madness that has dignified itself to call it normality, and the masses have progressed little farther than an orangutan, culturally and manner-wise.

These +mutations have assumed the destiny of uplifting the Earth in whatever way possible.

They act on a higher plane of reason and are gifted with genius energies that the ordinary would call delusion. For this reason, many will be thought mad or at least neurotic. It is their hidden action working for the salvation of the world. They are the active creators of a new order of the Ages.

Reprise (a poem at age 66)[18]

Darkness absorbing the sun
Much has been attempted
Little won
Afterglow of life has begun
Moon-silvered light in lieu shine so
"Gold" was lost
Long time
Ago.

Delbridge takes the stage at E. J. Thomas Hall. *Photo by Cameron Kaglic.*

Delbridge responds to applause following his performance at E. J. Thomas. *Photo by Cameron Kaglic.*

Jazz pianist Theron Brown plays an original piece written to accompany Delbridge reading "This the Poet as I See" at E. J. Thomas Hall. *Photo by Cameron Kaglic.*

Old friends Kevin Tucker and Walter Delbridge enter backstage at E. J. Thomas Hall, ahead of Delbridge's performance. *Photo by Cameron Kaglic.*

Book of Ideas

Book of Ideas

Each numbered topic to be developed by writing, analysis, action, speculation, practically, or other ways creatively.

January 3, 1982

1. The Effects of Ideas on an Unstable Self-System
2. Wave-Form Dynamic: Aesthetic Spiritual Action Levels
3. Structural-Level Communication Laws
4. On Personal Efficiency: Biologic, Psychologic, Sociologic
5. Psycho-Spiritual Levels of Love
6. Principles of Mental Evolution
7. Mind Associational Disturbances from Zonal Bodily Ills
8. Electronic Media's Impact on Unstable Personalities
9. Intrapsychic Disturbances on Eidetikers
10. Eclectic Psychotherapy
11. Degenerative Linguistic Habits and Behavior Problems
12. Faulty Body Image and Control in Schizophrenics
13. Bio-Computer for the Gods—A Story
14. Cosmic Dream Interactions—A Story
15. Moral Factors in Fate Determination
16. Clear Objective Visualization and Schopenhauer's Theory of Genius
17. Music Selection as a Way to Self-Development
18. Limitation and Self-Discipline

Idea Roots

1. Contributions towards a psychology of creativity and existential problem-solving cognitively and practically. Protocols for a group norm or situation. Role determination influencing actions.

2. I feel that I'm trapped in a zoo with a bunch of wild animals.

4. Drop the regnant categories of assessment. Explore inner transcription results.

9. The one Godspeeds, the other goes to seed.

10. I'm no longer interested in telling people myths and stories, but the hard and inescapable truth.

13. Today gaining knowledge is not a matter of egoic ornamentation, but self-defense against Poverty / Destructive Manipulation / Ravages of Nature / Pain from Poor Judgment.

16. One learns late or soon that books are not to everyone a boon.
    One learns late or soon that everyone dances to a different tune.

18. BE, not seem!

21.   In my mental isolation
              I BE
          The major sons of fortune
          Want nothing to do with me
          So I minister to music poetry
          Study life
          And write
          I'm poor but inwardly free
          Also
          Sure as can be
          In my poverty and reputation ruin
              Learn as I learn
              I, many still shun
              They think me nothing
              Without money or fun.

25. Personal competition: ugliest scar on social existence
        Co-operative unit: optimum integral growth and effectiveness

26. By trying to learn certain things I find my natural limits.

27. I'm trying to understand the vastness of God by studying the sciences.

28.   Resolve: Leave myth and fantasies far behind
        Get knowledge and wisdom
        The effective kind.

30. Imagination based on aesthetic reactions to facts.

32. Christians are always asking for forgiveness of faults they have no intention of correcting.

34. Those without much money in America have much to fear for the future.

37.   Feverish rush to disaster and tragic end
        Irresponsible hedonistic bend
        Burning life too fast
        They rush to Death
        Fearing that if they rest boredom will
        Begin again.

38. Many persons put up a "NO HELP WANTED" sign when it's obvious that their judgment is in bad disrepair.

46. Too frequent repetition dulls the edge of sensation—bad news for sensualists.

51. Philosophy and science are more fun than preoccupation with anger, fists, and guns.

55. I was depressed today. The sun and the moon went their regular way.

57. Put to flight the thoughts which bite into the mind at night.

59.   Childhood mind
        A hummingbird a rare find
        A railroad spike in a tyke's hand
        And summer flowers before a shower of
        Raindrops
        Pelt the
        Roof
        Of
        Our House

Where
Love makes me a
Happy
Child.

61. Present Earth is a terrible place where dreams get deferred, character gets slurred, and distinctions get blurred.

62. I believe that the form of creatures only allows small inklings of universal truth. Truth penetrates man but is not limited to each's limited perception of it. All creatures participate in truths, but are limited by form and functions: fish worlds, wolf world, in man the churl, commoner, the professional, the sensualist, the artist, scientist, as well as messengers from above degrees in between each type as the vision of Light alight. We exist in an ocean of Life ascending to Love.

64. That's not real life but veiled death.

66. Bequeathed to mankind's children a mushroom and atomic cloud persisting in error here and abroad. We, all of us to Einstein's horror if we do not speak out loud, will be consumed in fiery disintegration too fast to scream at mankind's fall we'll each and none of us need a shroud.

67.   Reproduction: Salmon struggling against the currents of streams
      Death: Lemmings rushing into the sea
      Absurd acts to human rationality

70. The only imagination helpful to life is that which shimmers truth and reality with beauty, significance, and meaning.

78. Destiny causality: Past actions leading to practical and psychological scenarios

79. Non-Attribution Identity Theory—an idea to be explored

81. If I say only what everyone else says, what have I said?

82. Karma as a secular process

83. Most people want you to be whatever they say you be.

84. Regardless of what we could have been, we are what we are within.

85. I started in youth with an optimistic grin not knowing that in maturity my ordeal to be would begin.

God, Musings, and Memories

March 24, 2001

1. Heal the wounds of time

2. Venerable age best when sage
   Experience used not lost
   Dignity achieved despite the worst.

8. Weep-steep-deep my lost love

32. Evolution got us to our bodies
   But the mind and spirit always outside the body

38. After trying very hard what happened is God's sovereignty predestined his own fate.

39. Fruits of memory from the alphabet tree

42. The Story of Many a Minor and a Major Discovery

43. Are you free to be destined decidedly?

45. Grace field between opposites

65. Life pattern discontinuity and mental illness

66. Teachers: Sketches from Memory
   Early, Middle, High School

67. Professors: Sketches from Memory
   Morehouse, Harvard, Yale, Akron U

68. "The Fathers" in My Life

69. Many Mothers, Sisters, and Brothers

70. Every Song Leads Back to the One

71. A Stranger "Handicap"

72. Doctors medical love known

73. Psychiatrists: Rescuers from "Shipwreck"

74. The Only "Solo" Act Belongs to God

75. Music: The Language of My Soul

76. Music—Mathematics—Greek Alphabet Sounds

77. Rose: Companion of My Fate

78. Time: From Rough to Refined, From Common to Sublime

Sun on Glass Lake

April 9, 2001

67. Of a not fully revealed plan, I write with pen in hand.

85. What does it mean to arrive at one's departure and destination at the same time—Chime me a ring of time.

Moonbeam Down Sliding the Rising of Life

August 2001

1. Time is the Archenemy of Idle Dreams.

2. Cleave to the truth. Against such measure the false cannot last long.

3. _____

ALABAMA CYCLE
    I. Birmingham Beginnings
    II. Boyhood in Tuskegee
    III. Reflections
    IV. By Bus to Akron
    V. The Trip through History
    VI. Arrive and Shaming and Fear
    VII. Uncle Carter
OHIO CYCLE
    I. Allen (School)
    II. Neighborhood at Miami Court
    III. At Shirley's House
    IV. Play
    V. Carter Takes Jimmy and Me
    VI. Bimbo or Aunt Anna's Shoulder
    VII. Miller School
    VIII. Boiled Horsemeat
    IX. "Zoo-Keeper" and Light Scientist
    X. Firestone Public Library Experiences
    XI. _____

4. A camper walked towards a skunk too late,
    Skunk raised tail camper stunk: Lysol y'all.

7. He was so hyped that when asked "A penny for his thoughts" he fancied himself a millionaire.

9. I have no real chimes in this life, but I will go on in radical counting every nothing the best decisions I can and bear anxiety and alienation with as much equanimity as possible at any given moment. I'm committed to Christ, but in social life, I'm an existentialist.
8-29-2001 Not Defeat Just Reality

11. I don't believe that it is honestly possible for a twenty-first century person to live by only one totalized and monolithic world view in a fragmented and complex world. Such monolithic philosophies may have been possible when there were only a few worldviews that competed for one's allegiance. Thousands of years of cultural opinions are now available in this complex computer-driven selector of I, with publishing casting up option after option. In a diverse divided world, monolithism seems in the least to lead to instability and inadaptability. Total consistency today may lead one to the madhouse, or marginalization, or even death. Sometimes mystic, sometimes Christian, sometimes, stoic, sometimes contingent existentialist, and so on. Said life seems to be a moving mosaic of many examples and moods. Single vision might be possible in a seated situation; today it seems to amount only to a fixed idea or system. Those with stable environments who associate only with their so-called "kind" may have the illusion that their way is the only way. That attempt for me has been shuttered repeatedly. I've been technically labeled insane as manic depressive. I don't choose the fragmentations of this time nor the all too evident emotional chaos of a copieth at odds with itself: I'm just the fall boy.

29. What I do is not for reward but necessity.

30. Dreams: The creative mirages of the mind

31. Listen to . . . Heart

32. Her Aura became yellow and shined so bright
        my sight was smitten by a divine love

35. Some wait, others have fun, some others worry and work.

36. A Philosophy of contingency amidst multi-possibilities

37. One can't live like hell and expect heaven.

38. Been through the "treatment" minimal expectations

39. One will never "know" enough yet decisions must be made.

40. I've a Christian soul but a Buddhist mind: In search of honest resolution

41. On relearning life at Fallsview Psychiatric

43. A United Nations Hospital: Universalism in Action

46. Getting a liberal education at Borders Books, Music, and Café

47. On churches and cardboard boxes: Relations

48. What it was like at first probate

49. Most people want peace but have trouble agreeing on how it is to be done.

50. "Objective Art" has profound effects on consciousness.

51. In "Objective Art" this artist concentrates certain universal essences.

52. "Objective Philosophy" not only exercises the mind in thought, but restores one's consciousness and the brain adding new "organs" to the mind.

53. "Objective Beauty" creates virtual experiential reality in the reading.
      Define aesthetic-conceptual experience

56. Real reality is governed by strict rules; if we go against such we pay in some degree.

58. All admiration for those who know how to do things

59. What's music to one ear is noise to another. All around the choice lost.

60. Differences are necessary strangely. Poor and rich thought and loved the same.

61. How can one save "face" when one has been effectively effaced
      Realizing one's own "nothingness"—build new foundation

62. The Man Who Doesn't Count: Zero Makes All Numerations Possible

63. Building a Foundation on Nothingness: A Difficult Miracle

64. My aunt and uncle told me I was "nothing." Jean Paul Sartre, an existentialist, says that consciousness comes out of nothingness. Supposedly god created the universe from nothing. Can a man build a self from nothingness?

65. I refuse other's hatred, can't use it; they must decide what to do with it. I'm not their "sponge."

66. Sound and Optimism, Moral Realism, Social Pessimism

67. After moist tears the soul bleeds.

68. Pray with every cell that others and self will be well

69. Father of Light illuminate our night

83. I was, I was crushed in 1987. I began at ontological implosion zero point. I am different. I am a conscious unit of humanity.

85. Every "TRAGEDY" tells us we're only human.
Why pretend otherwise only to further heartache?

87. Both Ape and Man love bananas. How about a bit of humility?

88. Sometimes linguistic habits are a truer sign of genetic makeup than any physical characteristics.

91. Real-Time Engagement Present-Moment
Comprehensive Livingness All Senses Alive

95. Scattered Spectrum of Souls
O Common Fathers—Endlessness on Earth and Beyond

96. Thou O Lord sustains all by the power of spirit. Objective prayer your language supreme whether waking or in lucidic dream.

97. Sol-Sun, Sole-Sun, Soul-Sun

98. Spiritually "crucified" without nails

99. I don't expect much from this world
Yet I will still work on as long as possible

100. Father Forgive! They don't understand!
For a long time I didn't understand myself

102. On seeing other's misfortune think—it could be me.

103. Turn and see the miracle of a tree

Touch Tones: Inner / Outer Working Insights: Neurocracy Old and New / Fragments of a Creative Path (May–June 2009)

6. "Straw dogs" bite the invisible only to be ever haunted.

11. The dawn of happiness can only be found in the Imagination.

13. Diverse ways and diverse people enrich our lives from stupa to steeple, from chopsticks to South American dance kicks. We were all made to see in color instead of the stereotypical black and white, the race and me.

14. Many a "Mad Man" has seen truths others were blind to.

15. Darwin, Marx, and Freud told truths about the so-called natural man, and it's rather disappointing. The reason for hope is that these men, as genius as they were, missed something. They knew nothing about the potentialities of the human spirit coming from a higher spirit to possess certain men and women to lift the others from the muck and mire of the present and past. Hope is future.

16. A "saint" is a so called "sinner" who attains reason, equanimity, measure, and realization of the natural humility proper to mankind.

17. A Venture
   God's so high and sovereign
   His ways I cannot discern
   Why my agony, I do not know!
   All I know is what is and what's so as I go:
   As it happens here below.
   Whether Heaven or Hell I go
   Such decision not left to me
   Cash registers jingle for someone else's prosperity
   Poverty and obscurity is left to me:
   Some call me a genius;
   Of that, I cannot say:
   But curses come my way each day
   While I struggle with the right way
   To go.

DESTINY, FATE, KARMA, PREDESTINATION
　　Some say.
　　After I die then I'll know;
　　But here below, only power, scheming, and corruption
　　Carry the time.
　　I,
　　Only a fool with a pen in hand,
　　Indict
　　The AGE!
　　Until miracle happens, I'll scribble, scribble away:
　　Hoping, The truth in Life,
　　I'll find someday.

18. At length he explained and explained: but the long and short of it was that I wasn't going to get my money.

19. After a life of sin, his choices narrow to three: become a resigned reclusive writer, an amateur scientist, or a ventriloquist of some long-dead saint.

22. Omnipresent electronics turn us all into vitalized ghosts.

23. I wasn't myself today: I was perhaps "you." Mirror.

25. A poultry-geist is an invisible cowardly chicken man.

26. A sighchic is a melancholy person with second thoughts.

27. She walks in beauty well-hipped. Chic-très hip, my girl walks on.

28. Writing is parasitic on a man's soul; so the same with religion.

29. The dead past lives on our life: so new generations will live on us, as we pass.

31. Trochée and trachea; poetic issue and organ-matrix of language

32. Asp and grasp—a snaky grip

33. Fee or free—to charge or not to charge?

34. Infusionism spasm—a holy fury

37. Stowed-away-run-away slaves

40. "Stoned" cuckoo birds obsessed by mechanical cats

41. Petrified Dignity—Mt. Rushmore

42. "Cat on a Hot Tin Roof"—sexual patter in a rain storm

43. My Love is a "Dove"—chaste for The Holy Spirit

44. A philosopher and his girlfriend—Platonic Love

45. At "Wits End" begins our introduction to wisdom.

46. The "duck" was stuck with a bill of inconsiderable size. Was he a "duck" or a "gull?"

47. Advice—given is almost useless: fools ignore it, wise men already know it, the mediocre only act on it accidentally and little remember who gave it. Maybe they thought of it themselves, a little plagiarism for self-improvement.

48. In "absentia" I impersonate myself: rather badly—I fear.

49. What is a ghost? A ghost is a "you" without a body.

50. A Holy Ghost is a most holy igniting contagion to shouting and mishmash utterances. A Most Holy Ghost leaves the congregation solemn, quiet and with adoration. Question, what is going on here? Ask your minister or priest but not me.

51. Maybe the world is not just about human beings and it's aiming at something different, something quite other. Maybe we are just the means and not the consummated end of it.

52. Look inward and up! Out and around has become habitual.

55. Autobiography of a childhood dunce—about myself. So they thought.

56. Driven to the life of the mind by the brutality of reality and the terrors of the unknown!

57. Insanity came when the MIND was unprepared for unexplainable MYSTERY.

58. Cleaving to the Divine. Human love and friendship with an active healthier mind brought real healing.

63. Voluntary servitude to the search for Truth will get no "Emancipation Proclamation" this side of life. One appreciates bare-life itself, and a few non-harmful pleasures, and supports all those strong enough to handle that "wild" mass called Humanity.

65. Some of my statements are paradoxical: the world is paradoxical, existence is paradoxical. Scripture is paradoxical. Anything beyond a one plus one equals two type mentality goes to paradox or metaphor. Is reality a great poem written in flesh and blood, storm and stress, anxiety and peace, sanity and insanity, truth and illusion? Would we rise up against this Cosmic Poet and demand a better part?

66. To the "normal" and "upright" I'm just social "refuse." I pray that God is more kind.

67. The philanthropy of a poor man drives him deeper into poverty, but not giving drives him towards inhumanity—small sum as it is.

69. Almost all of us are afraid to say that some things are no longer believable. Awaiting a fresh "INFUSION!" Only this will still the doubt, stop the confusion, and give me back my sanity.

72. Young boys losing their lives in old men's chess games of geopolitics under the weight of a world of old lies.

> Let us live and think of a new game. Perhaps we can keep a green planet, a live planet, a planet where people can have noncancerous skin enjoying the beach with hope for children again. These old men nearer death need not pull us down with their nether games of xenophobia, racism, chaos, and destruction. We must seek levity not gravity and rise above our history of leaded weight, of crime, exploitation, and greed. May those YOUNG MAKE A NEW BEGINNING and much hope from an elder who loves crayfish, flowers, fish, trees, bushes, and adventure in youth and still do so prosper.

74. I'm a stable artist. After years of being half insane suffered strain and pain, and treated cruelly and ridiculed—I'm back, stable again.

75. My mother said I was born during a fierce thunderstorm with torrents of rain falling down. She said I was a quiet baby. Psychologists say that quiet babies are abnormal. It's a wonder I survived so far; quiet babies are likely not to get fed by not crying. Only survival came with a good mother, tending to me as if by telepathy. I guess the psychs were right.

79. A statement of fact is a statement of fact. How can you improve on an empirical intuition? Imagine a new construction.

80. No booze, tobacco, thugs, or drugs—escaping debt and the "fuzz."

81. Too bad too bad, depression's a "monkey on the back" making one glum and too slow to act, something of a "sad sack."

85. Many "rags to wretches" story for a few "rags to riches" exceptions.

86. The most deluded are those "prisoners" who think they are free because they see no bars around them.

87. Most men don't wake up they screw up; women don't like that.

88. I was late for a date, so the contact was cancelled.

89. "Brand new you." "Brand new me." Same old story.

92. Falcons land with hooked claw, falconers wear gloves so no blood the falcon can draw.

96. Remember death! Then live, something may result from the effort.

97. Heaven! How can an earthly language speak beyond its circuit? Even Lazarus after Christ's resurrection of him spoke none of it.

98. Circles of hate form a repetition—zero—nothing positive.

100. "All's well that ends well…" One day I'll learn to spell while under a Spell—It might sell!

Untitled

36. From something to nothing to servanthood

38. Pressure doesn't always crush and destroy
      Sometimes it makes diamonds!

58. In a half moon haze, in an intimate daze

64. More is expected of any one man than he can actually live up to.

65. A dweller apart to protect a heart

68. Assume nothing, inspect—then decide.

73. Bless, bless the people and those who labor for them O God—Forgive me and restore my weight into light and leave this time's present darkness.

76. 4th Dimension of Transcendence: The poetry of loss

79. Astral travelers at reality's intersection

80. At the end of one's resources comes the comfort.

81. Once begun the web is spun—anyone for spiders?

83. Da Capo: Time intervals spiralic—same situations return.

84. He was a top in ideas—up-to-date dressed in old clothes.

85. Rustic—he gushed about god and goldenrods.

91. He outran himself to escape it as sowing memory.

99. Certain divines feed on mystical "moonshine."

100. A lost "Identity" finds a Self.

101. A bar, a staff, G-Clef and Scherzo laugh

106. He was true, not necessarily his followers.

109. Ghostic about existence, agnostic about what's beyond.

110. All that claims must be put to the test.

111. To be free from headaches takes the acid salicylic
       From a willow tree to make aspirin to have a remedy

112. By the "shrink" I've been "shrunk;" all loose talk of freedom is bunk.

113. You're only free to do what's allowed to you, or, take the bad consequences.

114. Free I sought to be, only to fall under necessity—psychologic economic tyranny.

115. Lack of money rules out certain desirable possibilities.

116. As far as secular life is concerned, economic issues are crucial.

117. Don't lie to the children—tell them they'd better study or end up in poverty and disgrace.

118. Ignorance is only funny to those not sunk by it.

119. Strange thing this scene of folks addicted to the obscene.

Soul Stages

24. It's apparent to me that souls have to be free to be.

Walter Delbridge and his notebook, at Nervous Dog in Akron, Ohio. *Photo by Miriam Bennett.*

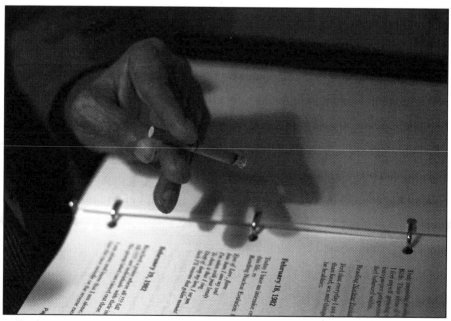

Delbridge reviews the first draft of his typed journals. *Photo by Miriam Bennett.*

Books Delbridge recommends from his library. *Photos by Miriam Bennett.*

From the 1982 journals. Delbridge writes much of his work on whatever paper is available, including the backs of old bank ledgers. *Photo by Miriam Bennett.*

Journal of a Reflective Poet

Excerpts from 1982[19]

Introduction

In 1982, Walter Delbridge moves from a small rented room near the interstate to his very own one-bedroom apartment down the street from Summit Lake. This newfound independence ushers in a thriving intellectual period. Channeling a vibrant creative surge, he is reading hundreds of books and writing nearly every day.

At age thirty-five Delbridge is developing an expansive—albeit pessimistic—worldview, which he attempts to integrate with his personal mission to "add something positive to the lives of others," even as he retreats further into isolation. He makes a brief return to graduate studies at The University of Akron, which he had left a decade earlier when his brother Willie was murdered. At that time, he was one of just a few at UA to receive a fellowship for graduate studies and was in the midst of a slow comeback, after being institutionalized several months at Fallsview Psychiatric for the diagnosis of schizophrenia.

By 1982, he's been in and out of mental institutions and continues to be on heavy medication that slows his thinking and dulls his creative vision. Yet he experiences intense bursts of inspiration which he struggles to balance, as in 1979 with the arrival of *Isolation and Intellect*'s 133 poems in a mere twenty-four hours. The 1982 journals are Delbridge's attempt to revive and revise his identity as a philosopher poet with a cosmic mandate. Still, he cannot find paid work and the pressures of physical reality plague him. His journals are a glimpse into the undeniable humanity of a willing and wildly open spirit whose depth of experience renders him vulnerable but not weak. His is a special kind of strength.

JANUARY 2, 1982
Reading *Architects of Fate* by Orison S. Marden (1897). The book is extremely valuable to me at this time. It gives much self-help aid and points out what others in the past have accomplished despite handicaps and setbacks. He stresses the value of honesty, hard work, resourcefulness, adaptability, and inventiveness. I believe that determination, hard study, and self-control will allow me to find some place in this society and to do some useful work. This book only makes it more clear to me that what I strive for is valuable regardless of how others see me. I'm aware of slumbering potentials in me which I must patiently study and develop. These potentials strive for expression, and I shall eventually give them expression in character, conduct, and belief. My primary sources of happiness are music, books, interesting conversation, writing, and creative productions. My studying too. Social contacts I hold a minimum. The research I'm doing is too valuable to me to sacrifice for mere idle chatter or discourses on other people's business. My field is not politics, but rather the concerns of the arts and sciences.

My experience has taught me that we pay in some way for every mistake and suffer for our ignorance. This is a very dangerous world where the majority have a hatred for any higher values and resent anyone attempting to rise above circumstance. Nevertheless, I must press on despite the dangers and all surrounding me.

JANUARY 3, 1982
Barry and Bobby finally got me moved into my new apartment at 359 W. Miller Ave. It is the best living quarters I've had since my birth. I shall take care of it and make the most of its design and compactness. Terry and Sue came over and helped me unpack and get settled in. I'm very pleased with the situation and have many plans for visits by friends and others who wish to converse with me. My thoughts keep going back to Louise, who's moving into my old apartment at 608 E. Buchtel Ave. She is beautiful, courageous, intelligent, and fun to talk with and know. I have to see what develops as time goes on.

Had a pleasant visit with Terry and Sue. I feel a certain closeness with them. We've gone through a lot over six years of knowing and visiting each other. We, all three, have had symptoms and sought therapy for our problems. Terry is growing stronger and surer of himself, and Sue is getting more emotionally stable.

Learned a great deal from John at 608 E. Buchtel. He's truly a disturbed genius. He has a photographic or eidetic memory especially on the semantic type. He brought up a great deal of specific facts from a number of fields. His instant habit of accuracy forced me to acknowledge my ignorance and learn the value of precision and accuracy and not just generalization. Intellectually we supplemented each other. I with laws, theories, processes, and generalization, and he with specific and concrete facts. I'm a better person from having known him. Some of his problems include lack of thoroughness in study—reading just paragraphs instead of whole books, obsession with his personal past, delusions of grandeur, self-centeredness, and general untidiness. All these faults are offset on the positive side by his love of learning, truthfulness, attempt at fairness to all races and creeds, and a desire to do good. All in all, eccentric, but a genius nonetheless.

JANUARY 4, 1982
This morning put in work order for stove to be fixed. Called Mr. Ross. He stopped by at noon. He brought a cake to celebrate my moving. We talked for two hours. As we talked, I got more and more disenchanted. He wants social change and so do I, but we differ as to how to get it. I think it has to come from the structures of society in planned controlled manner. He believes in an almost romantic idea of action by the rank-and-file people putting pressure on the status quo to make it change. I sense danger for me in all this. I've already received threats from "above" not to get in anything of this sort. Needless to say, I want to live. Anyway, I value what I may still do artistically and scientifically. Politically I'm not a rebel, and if I become one, it will be because I'm forced to do so and not by choice.

JANUARY 5, 1982

Call from Barry, he's trying to get some financial help until he gets another job. He's reading *The Rise of the Phoenix* by Christopher Hills. He doesn't have any transportation.

Call from Terry and Sue from her mother's house. They wanted to know what I was doing—will visit later.

Call from Mr. Ross. He expressed anger at society for what it's done to me and countless others. He wants to see a sane, nurturing, and free society. I told him that what I suffer is my personal fate, and I feel no regret for it. My only concern is for others who don't have the inner resources to cope with what's happening.

JANUARY 6, 1982

Read Encyclopedia articles "Creativity" and "Creative Thinking." Rereading Ernest Becker's *The Denial of Death*. Mr. Ross came by and gave me encouragement to keep researching and following the intellectual path. He has conversed with me intensively for over a year and half and has helped me regain perspective, balance, and a larger and deeper view of life.

I also read a book review by Benjamin DeMott about a book written by a radical psychoanalyst. The author is Joel Kovel, and the book *is The Age of Desire: Case Histories of a Radical Psychoanalyst.*

Also read *Community Mental Health: A Historical and Critical Analysis* by Bernard Bloom. Mr. Ross gave these to me to read.

Not feeling too well this evening—feel that my blood pressure may be up because of continuous nausea several times this evening.

JANUARY 7, 1982

Continuing reading *The Denial of Death* by Becker. What he's saying makes me more tolerant of others' defenses. Making me more humble and self-abnegating in regard to others' needs. Must remember at all times that in most cases people are the way they are because of certain problems in being secure in self-esteem. Be easier and more understanding of people. Make aware of the tragedy of life—an overwhelming realization of the vulnerability of people and the hells they create for themselves and others to escape fear. I'm feeling that I'm charged with the responsibility to help the poor, the outcast, and the disadvantaged. The question with me is when and how?

Fundamentally, I'm a researcher and theoretician but I have a sense of social responsibility despite the stigma society has placed on me as "mad."

JANUARY 8, 1982
Rereading *Living Philosophies* and finding that most of my feelings about life are scientific and deterministic. I believe that what a person becomes is an interaction equation involving the interplay of heart and environment. I believe in measure, the Golden Mean, and a scientific approach in general, softened by understanding and compassion.

JANUARY 9, 1982
No matter how you try to analyze life and control, it goes forth in diverse directions; it is a stubborn impulsive force. This is a note to all would-be tyrants.

Religion is a cry for justice, beauty, purity, and truth, but in our chaotic world it is powerless to bring these about. In order to get these things, we have to be realistic and work in the physical and social world to remedy widespread ugliness.

JANUARY 11, 1982
Mr. Ross called, and our debate or dialogue continues. He has ideas of man's basic goodness being spoiled by society and institutions. That seems too simplistic to me. Men often do self-defeating, futile, and stupid things. I'm non-idealist in this sense. I'm a realist who sees many complexities. I'm not taken in by glittering and merely hopeful ideas. Life is difficult and dangerous, and I'll do what I can to help people but not at unnecessary risk to my life.

JANUARY 12, 1982

Went to bank this morning then to the public library and got the following books:

1. *A Guide to Psychologies and Their Concepts* by Calvin Hall and Vernon Nordby
2. *The Philosophy of Santayana* by George Santayana
3. *Personality: Theory, Assessment, and Research* by Lawrence Pervin
4. *Men of Mathematics* by Eric Temple Bell
5. *The Golden Age of Science* edited by Bessie Zaban Jones
6. *A Treasury of the World's Great Diaries* edited by Louis Untermeyer

JANUARY 13, 1982

It is apparent to me that I must resign myself to aloneness until I can find others with similar aspirations. Barry Brown has been my friend since childhood years, and he shares some of my interests. He read *Nuclear Evolution* by Christopher Hills and has read some of the Gurdjieff and Ouspensky literature.

Reading *A Guide to Psychologists and Their Concepts.* With Mr. Ross today we met with Dr. Moorstein and Mr. Pontello. They sized me up, and what they saw, I have no idea. I know that what I do and say is scrutinized by these people: I have no defense. I have to go on alone. What they make of me I have no control over. I just have to realize the realities going on in society and make the best adjustments I can. I try to be as sane and rational as I can be. I must deal with others the best I can. I'm surrounded by rejecters, judgers, and criticizers. The psychiatrists and psychologists are the only ones who've tried to help me be myself. People whom I'll always love are my mother and a few friends. She has stood by me in times of trouble with faith in me. The following friends have also stood by me in times of trouble with faith in me: Barry B., Eric S., John G., Bill C., Ann K., and Mrs. Gibson. I've received encouragement or assistance from Akron and Kent Ohio librarians, from Dr. Frank T. Phipps and Dr. John Popplestone. From certain others I've received insults, willful misunderstanding, malicious gossip, and social ostracism. Twice my life has been threatened. I'm really alone and misunderstood, but I believe in truth and God and will go on. I'm thankful to Mr. Ross for befriending me.

JANUARY 14, 1982

I require much solitude to be happy with myself. Most people bore me with their talk about trivial things, or obvious things, or gossip. I want to always be learning either theoretically or practically. I'm more interested in books and ideas than personal things unless they have philosophical or psychological significance.

A woman's education doesn't matter as far as an affair goes, but if I was fool enough to get married, I would want an intelligent woman whether she went far in school or not.

Reading *The Philosophy of George Santayana*. I find that my temperament is similar to his. The classical love of natural beauty, the poetic feeling for life, skepticism about democracy, the skepticism about fixed codified beliefs, all this I agree in common with him.

From my vantage point life is the most important thing. No idea is worth dying for. All these high ideals of changing society have my sympathy and support, but I'm pessimistic for I know that the masses are lost in amusement and distraction and that most of them desire the same things that the rich have.

Reflections:
Any sane society would help all its members develop themselves to their full genetic potential.
Any sane society would utilize as much of the talent in the population as possible.
Any sane society would educate for species survival.
Any sane society would not be divided by racism.
Any sane society would aim for maximal mental health.
Such a society would make available to everyone the basic necessities for life.
Ergo: We do not live in a sane society USA 1982.

I'm attracted to fleshy full-shaped women.

I've decided not to father any children because it seems that respiratory and circulatory problems are in our genes from my father's side. I have nieces and nephews with asthma, and I suffer from high blood pressure. I won't take a chance I'm fathering a child into the world handicapped with a physical disability.

I feel for tender-minded people for I see the world process as ruthless and merciless in too many places. Nurses who hate sick people, teachers who hate children and other heart-wrenching scenarios in life. This earth is a bad place to be sick, weak, or powerless.

JANUARY 15, 1982
Regions of love, regions of awareness in the higher center of the self. Applied Platonism and swirl of stars in the Heavens above. Cornucopia of sharing and caring. Much love and visions of beauty.

Platonic veils of mystery are rent
The angels come
Heaven sent...
O love of splendor and form fit beauties given
I swoon with love my heart is shriven.

My soul vibrates to all finer things; coarseness is a bitter shock to my system even though I've gained strength to cope with it.

My soul is that of an artist, my mind that of a philosopher, and my body too weak to do all the things I'd like to do.

A lot of my sentiments can be found in the writings of George Santayana. Aesthetic sensibility is a cardinal requirement for my happiness. I'm quickly alive to beauty in all its forms, especially in the human female.

JANUARY 16, 1982
I place self-discipline high on my list of priorities. I've disciplined myself to get up early and to study. These two things allow me to be organized

and productive. I don't believe in wasting time, time is too precious. Most of the few friends I have sleep until noon—time wasted.

Reading *The Golden Age of Science* by Bessie Z. Jones. My interests have progressively shifted from the humanities to the natural and life sciences. I have a strong need to study structures and functions free from human emotion and prejudices. I find human prejudices and ungoverned emotions stupid and generally a nuisance.

Also reading *An Outline of Man's Knowledge* edited by Lyman Bryson.

I strive to get my brain to operate in a cool and flawless way with the information I absorb. Cool, clear, accurate, and efficient.
Cybernetics, Neurology, Objective Psychology, and Logics: A Synthesis.

A very strong desire to understand scientific principles and become a well-rounded generalist.

JANUARY 17, 1982
After a brief flirtation with physical science my interests went to behavioral and life sciences. I'm in love with life—the organic.

My view on politics simply stated:
No matter how it's done the best and soundest brains should rule. Life is too precarious, and the world is too dangerous to entrust it to second-rate minds. I believe in equal opportunity, but when the weeding out process has gone so far, the best brains should rule.

A quote from the famous businessman George Forbes:
"The only good system is a good nervous system."

A statement I made to a friend when I was seventeen:
"The only way to break out of a circle is to go off on a tangent."

Learning a lot from reading my set *of Encyclopedia Britannica.* I'm reading the articles which interest me from Vol. 1 on.

I believe in being kind to those who are weak, but at the same time we must cultivate those who are strong and intelligent from all classes of society. The earth cannot be managed, and the human race survive on the backs of invalids. Compassion for the weak, but not at the suppression of the gifted and strong.

No one in my family understands what battles I have to fight, my feelings or aspirations. Hell, I'm on my own.

I was born alone, I'll die alone—in between is the heartache.

Keeping the hours
Caught in the grips of Fate
Without pretensions I try to relate
A thankless task
Among those caught in illusions.

I hide my intelligence, dreams, and many truths from family and friends. There's much they wouldn't understand and I don't want to harm them in any way.

Most people are sensation freaks and hate thinking.

My physical appearance is a caricature and parody of my true inner being. I'm more masculine than I look.

JANUARY 19, 1982
As a body I'm frail and ailing and imperfect, but I share in spirit the dimensions of the human race high and low and I'm in harmony with the plants, stars, and cosmic rays as the Milky Way turns on its axis.
    I accept limits to feel the illimitable
    I accept rejection to experience acceptance
    I accept life to make death meaningful
    I accept poverty to be free as a human being
    My material failure is a triumph of the spirit
    My devotion is to Life and Humanity
    I need no other religion.

JANUARY 20, 1982

Slept a long time and got up at 10:00 a.m. Reading *Aquarian Conspiracy* by Marilyn Ferguson. It's cured me of my pessimism and inspires hope again.

Reading *Personality Dynamics: An Integrated Psychology of Adjustment* by B. R. Sappenfield. A good refresher on basic personality theory. Mr. Ross seems more interested in politics than psychology. My interests are just the opposite, so we disagree.

JANUARY 21, 1982

Became fully aware of my weakened position in society. Just trying to cope as best I can. There are a lot of external forces impinging and prisoning me that are really beyond my control such as racism, trying to get a job in a recession, and being a psychiatric patient.

JANUARY 22, 1982

Up this morning at 7:00 a.m. Reading *Ego and Instinct* by Yankelovich and Barrett. My perception of most humans is that they're mainly emotional and irrational.

I have the agony of having too many ideas that are in advance of this time. There's nobody I can talk to, and the ones I could talk to don't want anything to do with me. I'm alone really and must bear that burden of realization of which I cannot speak if I want to live.

JANUARY 23, 1982

Tired of reading, but there's little else I can do.

JANUARY 24, 1982

I've recovered my energy and interest for reading—must cultivate reasoning and eventually write.

JANUARY 25, 1982

Went to the library and got eight books and stopped at the drugstore and got my medicine. I'm reading *A Philosophy of Solitude* by John Cowper Powys. A very cheering, good book for my lonely sojourn. After finishing it, I plan to read encyclopedia article "A History of Education." Chief enjoyments are reading and listening to music. Too many conversations are mere idle chatter.

I live in ideas, and spirit to me is living the harmonies of ideas as they bear on human feelings and consciousness.

The happiness of traveling the harmonics of music and ideas is superior to any social pleasure for me.

To give people and their human nature a too rosy aura is to invite disillusionment and disappointment. Many are closer to the savage than the angel. Instruction and education are the things which make them half-civilized.

I want to see people do better, live better, and be treated better. But I see, much to my dismay, so many are in ways self-defeating. This is either through ignorance, ungoverned emotion, or deep-seated psychological motivation. I have offered a certain book to a person whom I knew would have grown from reading it. No, refused to read it. Refused to govern temper.

Talked on the phone with my mother. She fell on the icy pavement and hurt her shoulder. Needs money. There's no way I can get more money. She's lived in poverty all her life. My youngest sister needs money for shoes. I can only give her eighteen dollars. I don't mind. I'm poor too, but I have my mind, my imagination, and my books. Feel worried about the feebleness in this struggle for life, but there is nothing else I can do. Much pain living in a broken family, a poor family, a family with little education. I do what I can to ease their misery. Nature or God, whichever is true, gave me my gift in my mind and imagination, and for that I'm infinitely grateful.

JANUARY 26, 1982

Went to group therapy today and felt better after leaving. Loretta has a lot of life and made me feel aware ever again of the basic humanity and drive of people regardless of education. Wayne gave me a ride home and gave me some magazines.

Oh Lord, the peasants of the world bowed with pain, these human so human people in pain.

John G. came by, and we had a smorgasbord discussion ranging from American history to the Kabbalah. He was less overbearing and more even-tempered than usual. He brought me a paperback copy of Pascal's *Pensées*. After he left, I called my mother. She's doing better again after hurting her shoulder. After only going to the first grade, she did a good job of bringing me up—not flawless, yet damned good. She instilled in me a great thirst for knowledge and some basic law-abiding ethical principles. There are some bigots in this city on both sides who hate me, but I believe in what I'm doing and will press on with whatever friends I find along the way. I plan to be truly and uniquely me. I don't force myself on anyone. Those who like me for what I am I appreciate; those who don't—too bad.

Reading a book, *The Science of Art* a seminal work by an artist scientist.

I feel a brotherhood throughout the ages with all humanity—especially the creative ones—and feel debt of gratitude that such ones lived. My life is just a summation of all I've read, experienced, imagined, and inherited genetically. I'm not the result of any one idea, any one race, any one event; I'm a result of all factors forming a resultant of history I'm aware of and all cosmic forces affecting me since conception. Anything I might achieve must be referred to humanity, God, and the cosmos at large. There's nothing personal in it, period. I personally am just a cosmic unit summating universal laws and human experience. I hate egotism, even if in my ignorant youth I was guilty of it.

At thirty-five, sexually, I'm something of a scopophiliac. I enjoy talking with and looking at attractive women. The physical act itself is a minor thing. My greatest pleasure is psychological and spiritual. This is different from my younger years when I longed for and had intercourse with several women—most of them five to twelve years older than I was.

One of the least things I have any interest in is power over other people. In human relations, I'm a born democrat; in politics, I simply believe that those with the interest of the country as a whole should rule. Democratic human relations / aristocracy of abilities.

JANUARY 27, 1982 12:25 A.M. CAN'T SLEEP.

When I came into the world—screaming and protesting—I had no fine clothes, no job, no respectability, no money. At that time, I didn't even have a name. I'll always remember that fact no matter what happens in this dangerous and precarious life. Fate and evil ruthless people have deprived me of job, reputation, and all things that this society deems valuable. I only thank God for my present awareness, my thirst for knowledge, and my love of simple unpretentious humanity. I will never misuse my abilities to take advantage of anyone. I will never run anyone down to build up my ego. I will suffer in silence rather than lie and destroy my own basic nature. Each person desires life and happiness just as much as I do. Each person has just as much right to their kind and way to happiness as well as I do. My mission in life is not to astound or impress, depress or repress others. My mission in life is to overcome personal faults in myself first of all just as long as I live and try to add something positive to the lives others I meet, even if that something is that I've taken a bath and say "Hello." I will not prostitute my soul for either money or applause. That would be a crime that I'd have to answer to God for. Many human beings suffer frightfully and that suffering struck me to the quick massively eleven years ago. That sensitivity to suffering and emotional chaos caused me to have a massive and severe schizophrenic breakdown. Since then I've had to build a shield around my "heart" as daily I've had to witness ridicule of justice, mockery of truth, persecution of goodness, and oppression of the weak. God has given me a heavy burden to bear. What I can do is uncertain and life is short—may God be merciful.

Can't sleep 1:00 a.m. Took 400 milligrams of Thorazine to try to sleep.

Every gift of nature or God carries responsibility. I feel that I have tremendous responsibilities because of my ability. Sometimes I wonder how I've physically survived the pressures and strain on an overactive brain. I have artistic, philosophic, and scientific capabilities. Yet my mind has laws of its own. I'm constantly growing and being altered by all that I sense, think, feel, and experience, yet there's a block on my ability to use media to express these things. It's as though my mind has taken on a massive problem (you might say the working out of a spiritual equation). It seems to require massive sensory and data intake, its analysis and synthesis holistically occurring so that eventually it will yield a solution. How long it will take and in what form it will emerge I have no idea. I hope God will allow me to do something in a nonsensational way constructively before I die.

Awake 8:00 a.m. "The Introjector: A story of a man who identifies with humanities and humanity's complexity."

Most people are inherently conservative. They can't get used to one changing his name, not to mention his ideas.

How I tire of human emotionalism, subjectivism, and partiality. Each of these little clods of ego hating everyone and everything that wouldn't let them have their way!

> I've faced the serpent in my spine
> Fought the dragon in the chambers of the brain
> Distilled "light" from human sweat
> The journey has begun.

Friends and family are the last to know the deeps of our soul. Familiarity breeds underestimation.

Never before in modern history have the common people felt so helpless before the recklessness of politicians.

We're but leaves in a fall wind.

There is an area of physical and mental suffering that no doctor seems to be able to cure.

I seek to discipline my body to support the needs of my soul.

JANUARY 28, 1982
People upstairs partying at 2:30 a.m. Life for me can only be for me as seen by an artist and not as a scientist or a moralist.

Tonight I had an interesting conversation with the "Cheshire Cat" and disappearances on both sides was the inevitable result. A parable of talks with friends.

A heroic couplet
A young guy and girl
Facing the world.

Brainstorm: a flurry of headaches (daffynition)

Incurious abandon at the rise of hope.

Adaptability: Dancing to the beat of a different drummer on one foot.

My God is not human and has no corporal body save the entire Universe. It is one who spans the galaxies and interacts on sub-atomic levels with it down to the smallest levels. It knows us through and through down to the smallest thought and It can do without our praises. If we do so it is because such means something to us as humans. My God is a God of integration and intelligence. No images can be made of my God and It does not require us to bow down. My God is a God of all languages, all time spaces, all living things in the entire Cosmos.

Reading Wieman's *Methods of Private Religious Living.*

JANUARY 29, 1982
My taste for seclusion these past several years is a sound instinct. I have to clear my mind and strengthen my spirit for what I must do in the future.

Christ said, "We are all part of one another." There is sound sociological and psychological evidence of this fact. If everyone was made emotionally and intellectually aware of this, we would not have crime, insanity, alienation or racism. Poor people are more human in this respect than the rich and the privileged.

One race—human. One planet—earth. One purpose—life.

Have become increasingly aware that I am mystical philosopher and predominantly devoted to a life of contemplation.

JANUARY 30, 1982
The body should be a vehicle for spiritual realization in mortal life.

A taste of Eden, Life as it would be if the apple had never been eaten.

> A cascade of rainbows over a spherical wonder
> A splendor of spirit
> This a new birth

Even though I go deep on the study of relation, I try to keep a balanced attitude regarding the affairs of the external and social world. In my opinion, religion is the crown of the body of disciplines, and regards internal states, morality, and conduct. Obviously if one needs medical care, he should consult a physician and not a clergyman. Each area has its proper sphere and requisite importance. One must keep a balanced view and assign each thing to its proper place, and feel accordingly. I've never been able to understand one-idea people. Why must one either be a poet or a philosopher? Why not both and more besides that. Wholeness, not fragmentation, is my goal.

The soul is the discipline of the mind and the mind the body.

Fell asleep awhile and my dream was full of sex. I think my unconsciousness is trying to tell me not to get too "holy" and forget that I'm only human.

JANUARY 31, 1982

Balance is the key for me in everything I do. Ungoverned negative emotions are not only ugly and unpleasant, but work against the health of the person experiencing them. Calm and balance should be the goal.

Broke away from reading *God's Design for the Ages* to read *How to Live 365 Days a Year* by John A Schindler, MD.

Everybody has memory tapes of drama-clusters. I experience life as a most interesting drama without any attempt to act or dramatize. It just happens that way.

I don't look on this period of my life as unproductive, but see it as a preparation for some socially useful work in the future. I eat one meal a day and sleep six hours.

Status congruence, simplicity, multi-strata relationships.

I've lived alone now since 1977 and I've grown, improved myself mind and body and like it.

Society has cast me in a role I don't like, but by my lifestyle I'm trying to make the best of it. I'm not a defeatist or a quitter. Ride the changes.

He was a fox in a tuxedo—medicine in one hand, poison in the other.

My semi-isolation is not because I don't like people, I do. But H. G. Wells said, "The future is a race between education and catastrophe."[20] I am trying to educate myself so I can do what little I can to avert some of many things pointing towards catastrophe.

Reality is no game and the laws governing it are grim. I've decided on my path and I plan to pursue it with diligence regardless of standing or misrepresentation.

Poetic and literary things need to be filled out by spiritual and scientific foundations. The sciences and the humanities are necessary for understanding man. I have drawn from diverse realms of study and my understanding grows apace with this process. Formal education only gave me the tools and resources for learning, the rest I've done on my own. Learning for me is a pleasure and the chief staple of my happiness along with appreciation of music, literature, and art. I also enjoy nature and good conversation.

Finished reading *How to Live 365 Days a Year.* Excellent book.

I haven't found yet the one thing useful for me to do. Until I do, I will keep studying and trying to improve my character.

Subliminations develop higher senses and regions of being.
An increase made of shade and sorrow.

FEBRUARY 2, 1982
I'm a union of a number of opposites.
Progressive sublimation into metaphysical love.
I believe that we're just cells in an Astronomic God.
The spiritualization process continues.

Reading *The Omega Seed* by Paolo Soleri. It offers great pregnant insights.

FEBRUARY 3, 1982
Finished *The Omega Seed.*
I'd rather underestimate than overestimate myself.

All the evils of the ages afflict our times. Certain people seem never satisfied with what I do or am. How much do they expect of a man who had a massive nervous collapse eleven years ago. All things considered, I think I am doing good.

I have to get more and more knowledge and self-discipline to stay relatively sane in a relatively insane society and world. Such things as: cruelty, gossip, malice, war, egotism, rumors, poverty, racism, oppression, bad language, ugliness, greed, competition, poor housing, hard-heartedness, mass ignorance, murder, crime…
A sane society would have little of these.

I'm taking the potassium chloride that Dr. Green has prescribed for me. I feel better and don't have the nervous twitch in my left hand. I also hope that it will help bring my blood pressure down. Monday my pressure was 130/90. Too high.

FEBRUARY 4, 1982
Heard on the radio that Martin O. Chapman is dead. I was remembering as far back as Thornton Jr. High School when he was Assistant Principal. He was indeed a scholar and a gentleman, and he always urged me to be the same. He was a good and kind man. All his life he showed regard for others and worked for the good of the Akron community. I regret his death and honor his memory.

Mr. Ross is at a turning point in his life as a result of reading *Psychological Reflections on Gurdjieff and Ouspensky.* He has a wealth of knowledge and experiences to draw on his search for higher consciousness, but he has a fear of giving up his constant involvement in active socio-political adversarial issues.[21]

Transportation gets us from one place to another, but what kind of consciousness is driving and being driven across town?

Spirit: Address Unknown—A metaphysical collection of reflections to be written.
The Vibration Registrant—A psycho-spiritual novel to be written.
Cortex Pointe—A meditation on brain functions in higher consciousness.

Just finished reading *The Handbook to Higher Consciousness* by Daniel Keyes. Book clarified much that I have been seeking for twenty-two years. Non-applause-oriented work for growth could bring health, sanity, and peace.

State condition affinity—a means of overcoming aloneness.
I cry not with water, but with anguish of the spirit.
My only aim is to become a corpuscle of love amidst humanity.
My journal and me, God, Life, Infinity, truly trying.

The only true Being is the Holy Spirit. We humans are only transmissive corpuscles of this divine energy.

The tournaments of the Superpowers are anti-human, anti-God and anti-Life. Get rid of the bombs!

I'm reading *The Labyrinth of the World* by John Amos Comenius and it shakes me to my foundation. I'm a cosmic mystic and love God and mankind.

Jesus is my ideal, not the clench-jawed warring militarist.

Music: Heartthrob of my life.

FEBRUARY 5, 1982
St. Paul: "Things of the spirit are discovered by the spirit."[22]

John Keats: "Life is a vale of soul making."[23]

FEBRUARY 6, 1982
Finished reading *The Labyrinth of the World*.

Read rapidly a small book *The Creation of God* by Joseph White.

I use knowledge and experience to grow a soul. The secret of spiritual growth is to make self zero and God—universe infinity.

Maximizations of potentials regardless of circumstances.

Reading *Human Energy* by Teilhard de Chardin, and I feel at once in step with his mode of thought.

Bodies are many, the songs of life are One
Spirituality united the man to the One.

My thought and being so complex, operating on so many levels difficult to express in language. Holistic, totalistic, emphatic, creative-organic.

Not to shine before man, but stand towards God.

To me books are not dead words to be memorized, but a participation in the living spirit of the author.

I know I can't be perfect, but I can try to live up to the best of my abilities. I feel I must strengthen my body to support the growing spirit within me.

FEBRUARY 7, 1982
My primary studies at this stage are science and religion. Especially mysticism and bio-social science.

Finished reading *Human Energy* and now understand what I'm trying to do.

Reading the The *Activation of Energy* by de Chardin. I'm just beginning to grow.

Scientists are discovering the order and the beauty of the universe while politicians are threatening to blow us all up. The future holds mushroom clouds or the first starship.

Beginning to read *The Thought of Teilhard de Chardin* by Emile Rideau.

Spiritually and emotionally this is the most painful period of my life. I'm unable to meet all the emotional demands on me and prepare for my future work at the same time.

Stopped reading de Chardin book and turned back to reading of *Science for the Citizen* by Lancelot Hogben.

I like Teilhard de Chardin because he unites science and religion.

Science for the Citizen: a big fat outdated book.

Reading *An Introduction to the Study of Man* by J. Z. Young. Too technical. Could not understand it.

FEBRUARY 9, 1982
Had a good therapy group meeting. Feel like I have become more fully human, emotionally as well as individually.

John G. came by and we discussed crystals and gems, physics, and other things. It was a learning encounter as usual. He stimulates me to grow more accurate and precise in my knowledge and calls out a host of facts stored in my memory. It's valuable knowing him.

FEBRUARY 11, 1982
Reading *Moral Society: A Rational Alternative to Death* by John David Garcia.

Finished the *Moral Society*.

Reading *A Sense of the Cosmos* by Jacob Needleman.

I'm convinced that there are higher regions in my mind, and I steadfastly search to make contact with them... I do not talk loosely of these things.

The world military confrontations and power build-up strike me as terrifying.

FEBRUARY 12, 1982

There are higher thoughts than ordinary thoughts and different emotions than ordinary emotions. The life of the ordinary and conventional person is an impoverished life.

Finished reading *A Sense of the Cosmos* and know that I'm on the right path in seeking higher consciousness and transcending this mere ego.

I'm reading *Personhood: The Art of Being Fully Human* by Leo Buscaglia. His discussion of Taoism makes me aware that I try to live a non-conflictive, unattached mode of life. My way of life results from many teachings and many philosophies. I try to be sincere and natural from the inner core of my being and I don't try to impose on anyone, yet it is my guide in every encounter. Serenity results from letting go of ego and egotism and being simple and sincere while being aware of the infinite complexity of life and relationships.

I am seldom lonely.

FEBRUARY 13, 1982

Today I am depressed and in despair. It becomes harder and harder just to physically survive, and most of the little conversations I have with others are obvious. I question why I should go on living and what value human life can have in the crazy world we live in.

FEBRUARY 14, 1982

I slept off depression.

Barry B. is a friend. I've known him for a long time and we can have discussions including creative and imaginative encounters. I value talking with him at this particular time.

Reading *The Right to Create* by Judith Groch. It is an interesting book with a balanced outlook on creativity and education.

Finished *The Right to Create*. Easy reading (3 hours).

Reading *Art and Belief* by Henderson (1 1/2 hours). A sensitive portrayal of modernization and beliefs in the twentieth century. Worth reading.

Reading *Insight: A Study of Human Understanding* by Bernard Lonergan—a big important book. It makes one think about thinking and understand about understanding.

I find my joy in reading and thought and music and imagination.

Feb 1st my doctor put me on potassium tablets and I feel much better as if something within has been replaced.

FEBRUARY 15, 1982
Woke up at 7:00 a.m. refreshed.

The threat to the world of nuclear and biochemical war can make all seem but futile options. Everything that I do has a touch of the unhealthy in the face of that doom possibility. How can we do anything in the face of this possibility of total species extinction? It's a damnable situation. When science and technology bring the world into the most widespread and intensive communication which should lead to a world culture, the world leaders threaten to end the whole human race with nuclear and biochemical war. A damnable situation.

I believe that I'm more of a Hindu or a Buddhist than a Christian. Christianity is not as spiritually nourishing to me as Hinduism and Buddhism.

The Loners: A Story
I've come to the point where I must make some sense of life going on around me.

Had a good conversation with Billy W. and Barry B.

FEBRUARY 16, 1982
Went to group therapy and it was fair. Flo's doing better, as well as Dwayne. Loretta and I have the problems.

FEBRUARY 17, 1982
Read selections from Sacred Swami Vivekananda. Truly inspiring reading. I get more from these Hindus and Buddhists than from the Bible. Their ideas of God and reality seem purer and truer than the Hebrew ideas. I feel myself growing deeper and stronger within, and much in everyday life falls into proper perspective. I'm developing a strong center of peace and calm and feel balanced within.

Reading *Nuclear Evolution* by Christopher Hill for the second time.

Feel that every day I am refining my awareness more and more. There's more to life than food, sex, and things.

FEBRUARY 18, 1982
Today I have an intensive certainty that I have lived before and will live again after this life.
Reading *Nuclear Evolution* further confirms the above.

Eyes of love flame
Into them I aim my soul
I'm taken with your beauty
To choir it thus I sing
Deep O deep my love I see you
Such I'll treasure that golden moment

FEBRUARY 19, 1982
Reached a point where all categories fail.
All there is is individuals with their individual importance and individual idiosyncrasies. No group label can cover over these rich differences which are sometimes tragic.

I am alone and know that I am alone. Any sympathetic smile is appreciated. I won't buy the race swindle or the reverse race swindle. All there is is individuals.

Reading Arnold Toynbee's *An Historian's Approach to Religion.*

Mystics with their talk of love of God. I can love creatures, but I have no contact with a Creator to my knowledge.

Finished reading Toynbee's book.

Peoples' slowness of thought and simplistic reasoning is a pain for me. I speed faster than words with penetrant intuition.

FEBRUARY 20, 1982
Objective sanity has nothing to do with statistical "normality."

Principles of psychological alchemy—self-transformation

Progressive sublimation and finer senses develop.

This body is the root, the mind the leaves, the spirit the forest.

Finished *Nuclear Evolution.*

Stratographic levels of reality: vibrational level resonance

Things I want in life take nothing from anyone else. Knowledge, solitude, the appreciation of music and beauty in all its forms. I'm not competing with anyone else, just autonomous and needing to realize my inherent potential at no one's expense. I'm paying the price for what I'm getting in poverty, loss of reputation and semi-isolation, but it's worth the price.

FEBRUARY 21, 1982
Reading *The Metaphysics of Modern Existence* by Vine Deloria, an erudite American Indian who is a great writer and makes an argument for non-Western wisdom.

Read only parts of Deloria's book and finished it.

Reading *Science, Religion and Reality* edited by Joseph Needham. Read the book in a quick cursory manner.

Whatever God is, He or It is not personal: A belief

Precision is necessary for moving bodies from place to place
But not for moving spirits from grace to grace.

Reading *Religion Without Revelation* by Julian Huxley.

Science and Religion are beating within me. Science is winning.

It's better in practice to assume that others soon tire of you, than that they're overjoyed with your presence.

FEBRUARY 22, 1982
Had a good discussion with Eric S. about social problems and individual behavior. He is intelligent and intuitive, but mentally lazy. I tried to convince him to study.

Finished reading *Religion Without Revelation*.

Read *The Encyclopaedia of Ignorance* especially the essays on memory, learning, and the brain.

FEBRUARY 23, 1982
Woke up at exactly 7:00 where the alarm had been set.

Reading *Issues in Science and Religion* by Ian G. Barbour.

Finished reading book by Barbour.

FEBRUARY 24, 1982
Man as a physical organism is nothing but a bundle of habits.
Society is misreading habit patterns.

The only freedom is freedom of the mind and spirit.
Physical and social determinism.

Science for the outer physical and social existence
Religion for the inner and individual
Never the twain shall meet.
Beginning to get a bias for the real and perceptible.

The world of contemplation is joyous and serene
The world of action is fraught with danger and frustration.
I prefer contemplation and will act only reluctantly.

Descartes epitaph was:
"To live hidden is to live well."
Those are the exact sentiments about my life. I wish to reveal myself to
others, but they don't have the intelligence or experience to know me,
and their egos keep them talking about themselves. They show little
interest in me as a thinking being.

I am beginning to think that beyond matter and sensualism, man can
know nothing. I've read scores of philosophies and religions, but nev-
ertheless have to cope with the everyday world as if I have read not a
single page. Others could care less about my "knowledge."

FEBRUARY 25, 1982
I've resolved to go my own way regardless of the misapprehension of
others.

I only require six hours of sleep and one meal a day.

My conversations with Mr. Ross have sharpened my intelligence, helped
me clarify my values and deepened my understanding of psychology.

I continually fight to master myself and strengthen my mind and spirit
in order to cope with chaotic life.

Too much time, money, and other people's hope have been invested in me to fritter away and waste my life. Right now I have no job and can't get one, but I will study and prepare myself with diligence and discipline. Eventually some kind of chance will come to me.

Music and books, music and books—my Paradise.

I'm too busy living my own life to meddle in other people's business.

These black men inspired me in my youth: Vernon L. Odom, George Miller, and Dave Wilson. I also got encouragement from Clifford Gates and Dr. Eldridge T. Sharpp. Too many people have assisted me in my development for me to waste my life and time.

People waste their time and life in foolishness and complain that they're not free. There's no freedom for the foolish. Their own habits and thoughts forge the manacles that bind them.

I've never felt a slave or agreed to being one regardless of others' attempts to make me one.

The real revolution begins at the nearest library, not shouting in the street.

I can never be enslaved, only imprisoned or killed, and I'll try to avoid both.

It seems to me that only a few principles are needed for a decent life:
1. Respect others' rights to live in their different ways.
2. Develop one's abilities to the utmost without egotism.
3. Use language in a civil and decent way.
4. Be positive and life-affirming rather than negative.
5. Take care of one's business and bills to the best of one's ability.
6. Do not gossip and meddle in people's personal affairs.
7. Obey the civil laws.

8. Accept oneself without the need to compare oneself with others.
9. Have a love and respect for nature.
10. Don't pass too easy judgment on others. There are physiological and psychological reasons for people's behavior.
11. Try to stay clean in body and mind.
12. Don't be a fool about sex—use it only as one part of life for perspective.

The white bigot and the black bigot are equally bad.

Civilized and intelligent people respect diversity, individuality, and character.

We are all being swept into misery by a ruthless world process.

My life and experiences are so complex, I despair to ever attempting to explain myself to anyone.

FEBRUARY 26, 1982
I cannot afford fantasies and daydreaming. The realities and dangers that surround me demand that I be realistic and awake.

Read *A Primer of Freudian Psychology* by Calvin Hall.

I live a one-sided life (pursuit of knowledge) and this is partly because of a love of knowledge, and the fact that I can't find a job.

Racism cramps and warps my life.

Society at large is a one-eyed cyclops with its glance backward tyrannously set against beauty and truth. I don't like and don't trust it. It's hurt me too much.

I don't believe in masses or classes or groups; I only believe in individuals.

There may be safety in numbers, but there's also tyranny.

When many people talk of community and altruism what they mean is that the individuals' actions and beliefs should be tyrannized by the group. If each man lived with some reason and looked after his own business properly, and daily allowed others to do the same, things would be better. Cooperation, but not suffocation.

At heart I'm an artist. no matter what other kinds of books I read and study. My vision of life is that of an artist, and my concept of God that of a Supreme Artist.

Read article in May 1961 *Horizon* entitled, "The Romantic Revolt"— rekindled my artistic aspirations, explained to me why I feel differently from most around me. Also read an "Interview with Ionesco"—he is outrageously creative and perceptive. The two articles stimulate me to take up the reading and study of literature again. Read the *Encyclopedia Britannica* (1980) entry on Samuel Taylor Coleridge.

Read *Time Machine* by H. G. Wells. Wells has been influential in my spiritual development. His clear thinking, realistic appraisal, and depiction have been inspiring to me. He was aware of man's promise, as well as his collective stupidity. He was a thinker of depth, clarity, vision, and deep humanity. Reading him has taught me to be realistic, incisive in thought, and cautious but purposeful in action. The story by him that impacted me most was "Star Begotten."

FEBRUARY 27, 1982
Every individual is a unique trial made by nature.

Most throw that unique practice away for some collective stupidity. In everything I do, I feel a tremendous feeling of responsibility.

From *Time Machine* by H. G. Wells page 74:
"It is a law of nature we overlook, that intellectual versatility is the compensation for change, danger, and trouble. An animal perfectly in

harmony with its environment is a perfect mechanism. Nature never appeals to intelligence until habit and instinct are useless. There is no intelligence where there is no change and no need of change. Only those animals partake of intelligence that have a huge variety of needs and dangers."

Phenomenological imagination allows one to experience multifaceted levels of experience.

Read partially *The Seven Mysteries of Life* by Guy Murchie.

Philosophy of an Artist—Projected Book
1.   Feelings and Regions of Awareness
2.   Purified Emotions
3.   Reactive to Sensations
4.   Metaphysical Musings
5.   Erotic Overview
6.   The Magnetism of the Unknown
7.   The Aura Around Particulars

For better or worse nothing is accidental.
Everything is ordained.

FEBRUARY 28, 1982
I find a bit of paradise in common things. A matter of imagination.

Terry called this morning and said that he and Sue never wanted to see me again.

My lot: Mockery, slander, persecution, and ostracism.

MARCH 1, 1982
Re-read *From Cretin to Genius* by Serge Voronoff.

Read *If You Don't Mind My Saying So: Essays on Man and Nature* by Joseph Wood Krutch.

The Heart: Techno Ant Heap—a play or novel to be written.

Electro-Vibrational Spinning—essay, play or novel.

Electronics, computers and behavioral technology have turned all of us into reactors and predictable ones at that.

MARCH 8, 1982
Technology is built for robots, not organic bodies.

Human beings are intermediary experimental subjects of higher non-organic beings—speculative idea.

Without God or gods or higher beings to bring to order man's affairs, mankind is doomed. Everyday news broadcasts make this abundantly clear. Man is too primitive and uncontrolled, mentally and physically, to rightly live in a technological society.

MARCH 9, 1982
I've resolved to push my discipline of reason to its furthest point.

After reading all these philosophies and religions, I find that I am really a stoic with both regard for measure and reason. Philosophic growth entails an agony of the soul. The body seeks to weigh one down to the sensual and mundane.

The curve of a bird in flight
A dancer in tights
Stars above at night
Worship under a budding dogwood tree

MARCH 10, 1982
12:30 p.m. Walking back from the bank I started retching and throwing up some nauseous effluvia that seemed to have invaded my throat. Have been throwing up for the last fifty minutes.

Transcendental Ethics—To be written.
1. Unit Integrity
2. Life Stream Ubiquity
3. Psycho-Ecologic Interdependency—Dualistic Paradoxes
4. Metaphysical-Genetic Straight-Dynamic Indices
5. [Illegible]
6. The Descent of Consciousness
7. Psycho-Physical Integration Necessary to Bear Consequences
8. Honesty as Simplicity Cardinal

MARCH 12, 1982
Read *Vendetta for Modern Man* by Christopher Isherwood.

MARCH 13, 1982
Reading *Of Time, Passion, and Knowledge* by J. T. Fraser.

Read encyclopedia articles on Aristotle and epistemology.

A feeling of anger not having people I can talk with on my own level and at being surrounded by unaccountable and primitive people in a body-obsessed and degenerating society. In my life, I control anger by taking tranquilizers.

I feel a stranger in this society. I live hidden. I live unknown.

Increasingly my only companions are books.

People's limitations imprison us.

Realization is a lonely journey.

A refusal to engage in futile battles.

The only way I can deal with most people is by taking heavy doses of tranquilizers.

Seagulls wildly flying over furrowing waves.
Bathed in the spray
Nature's winged denizens joyfully at play.

MARCH 14, 1982
Read *Encyclopedia Britannica* article, "Analytic and Linguistic Philosophy."

Today started to quit smoking.

Read some essays, "Tomorrow and Tomorrow and Tomorrow" by Aldous Huxley.

Helped my sister over the telephone do her homework.

John G. came by for two hours and brought me some philosophical essays.

MARCH 15, 1982
Life stampedes, hoof-hoofs, here come the horses.

MARCH 16, 1982
Cages of susceptibility stifling life.

I have an understanding of the necessity for order and law.

Reading *Readings in Philosophy* edited by John Herman Randall.

I seek to transcend my physicality and become a metaphysical being. The necessities of subordination are just that, in necessities for biological life. I find that the mind and the spirit are my true home. In my youth I had enough sexual exploits to last me the rest of my life. I'm moved more now by a spiritual and individual compulsion rather than a physical or sexual one.

Inwardly I'm moving at a fast rate. Many strike me as halting or going in slow motion for the most part.

I have joys and sorrows I can share with no one.

I understand many, but few understand me.

I complexify each day and move farther away from the statistically "normal."

My journey is a solitary one fraught with hidden love and hidden pain. Others silence me with their egotism and self-concern. I must commune with the sages by reading them.

The only answer to the obvious is silence.

Many futilities masquerade behind big words.

MARCH 17, 1982
Metaphysical children on a hedonistic spree. Under the strain of city and civilizational pressure many people are becoming sensualistic and aggressive animals with no moral guidance or self-control. The animalization of man in the cities increases as technical accuracy and media pressures step up.

MARCH 18, 1982
Finished *Fragments* by Paolo Soleri.

Quickly skimmed *The Next Development of Man* by Lancelot Law Whyte.

These times are too noisy, too chaotic, too primitive.

Read *The Essence of T. H. Huxley* by Cyril Bibby. Found it refreshing and inspiring for clearness of thought and the promotion of observation and accuracy in living.

People are being transformed into a consumeristic automatons to keep a blind production and money economy going.

MARCH 19, 1982
Read *Encyclopedia Britannica* article "Poetry."

The tension between my intellect and my feelings is intense.

Read *Britannica* article "The Novel."

Searching for suggestions and aids to battle writing block.

Every man has his own brand of anguish.

MARCH 20, 1982
This society is horrible to intelligence especially if the person is poor. He's forced to be concerned with thoughts and things he has no natural concern for.

MARCH 21, 1982
Core Registrant—Eideto-geometric romance to be written.

Despite education, despite culture, despite all, whites see me as a black man and consider me with the rest of the race. There's no escaping this and all that it entails. I don't make a very good slave. I resist servitude and slander on my personality by those who know nothing of me.

Society is based on lies and cruelty. The less I have to do with it the better.

Read *Listening with the Third Ear* by Dr. Theodor Reik.

Read some writing in *Theories of Counseling and Psychotherapy* by Patterson. It clarified a number of things about my problems and fears and inhibitions and has given me some ideas on how to resolve some of my conflicts. The problem is though, that even if I became one of the sanest men in the world, the general society remains troubled, strife-torn, addicted, hate-filled, crime-ridden, and so on. All that my efforts to become strong and stable can do is help me better to survive in a "real" society and though it's unlikely perhaps help bring about a better state of things.

MARCH 22, 1982
Repression acts as an impediment or blockage in the movement giving rise to synapses. Computer analogy—blocked circuits—shorts.

John G. came by and I was able to buy a complete *Bartlett's Quotations* book from him for two dollars.

MARCH 23, 1982
The deeper self is more real than all the phases of the self.

I've got my reasons for living the way I do and they are damned good reasons.

Earth life is the caesura between two eternities. Just by being a physical being in space involves one in problems and sorrows that at times seem positively senseless.

Beset by a host of troubles in the saṃsāric sea of multiplicity.

MARCH 24, 1982
I keep silent. It's not even safe to talk about elementary things, not to mention recondite matters.

Different languages place thought in different comprehension regions. Value space phenomenology.

It's better to pay immediately for one's errors or mistakes, get them out of the way, learn and go on.

My debt to things past and present is too deep and expansive to summarize them all. I've read over two thousand books in my brief lifetime so far.

Though I read much I still can't think freely…

Socially and psychologically, I'm abnormal at times.

My color does not determine me; it's just an incidental of my make-up, more important to others than to myself. Humanity is one species, man one race.

Cleanse the heart, strengthen the mind, purify the body.

Aesthetic Psychology—book to be written.

The suffering of the historical process. Suffering due to the chances of fortune.

Interpretative schematics imposed on perceptual traumas.

They should be subjected to a number of challenges if for no other reason than to drive home the point that life is not guaranteed and constant adjustment and readjustment is the path to evolution.

I'm scared, but I try to look at changes in fortune with an impersonal mind and impassive face.

How much misery is caused by defective thinking?

What the world needs is men and women who summon up intellectual history in themselves to create the future.

Schemas of dynamic cognitive efficiency regulation.

MARCH 25, 1982
As long as there are "winners" and "losers" there'll be psychological problems and human misery.

Finished reading *Reflections on Human Nature* by Arthur O. Lovejoy.

Read *Britannica* article on "Mind, Philosophy Of"

From *Bartlett's Quotations*: James Beatties (1735–1803)
"The Hermit," "He thought as a sage, though he felt as a man."

Reality is a cold mistress disappointing to hot and heedless lovers.

Nobility born of desperation in necessity given an oration.

There are ugly truths I have to live with that out of kindness I don't divulge to others lest they lose hope and pine away in despair or share a madness too painful to be borne.

Life has hassled us with roughness and given little of a damn about the sensitivity of the instrument.

If most people tried to live under the circumstances I live under, they'd collapse.

My intelligence I owe to the imaginative working on the sinews of experience. My ignorance I owe to the limitations made by my destiny.

That hurt and haunted look of a man who's seen too much truth.

Reality has horrors that make the imagination recoil.

After living thirty-five years I find few matters to joke about.

Modern American society is a manufactory of madness.

Society will poison a sensitive mind dram by dram.
Call it crazy not giving a damn.

I know others are suffering, but I can only speak for myself. Social action for me spells my death. I've already been warned by certain representatives of the state to stay out of politics or social issues. For me personally, I'm living in a totalitarian society. The methods have not come to outright torture or internment camps, but by psychological manipulation and economic threats the tyranny's still there.

Action requires money, and socializing. I'm poor and don't like crowds. I read things, listen to music, and have a few friends.

Relationships with women are largely a matter of money, indirectly or directly.

I shudder to think of all the bad things attributed to me by certain others, while I sit alone in my apartment reading.

Simultaneity is not causation.

The heat from the building melts the snow. It runs from the roof and trickles down below.

Afterthought is sometimes repentance of what went before.

Dreams give the action I fail to get during the day.

MARCH 26TH, 1982

1:00 a.m. After urinating I had sharp pains in the groin. It could be prostatitis again or the after effect of taking a lot of medicine and drinking coffee a lot. I'm not too happy about my health at this time. I take two blood pressure medicines, two kinds of tranquilizers, and potassium chloride. I have flare-ups from the prostate, high blood pressure, and insomnia. Hoping that I can get all the things under control and be at least tolerably well. The geneto-urinary problems are the worst. It ruins any possible sex life I could have.

Reading John Dewey's *Human Nature and Conduct.* His writing clarifies my thoughts and saves me from useless abstractions. He is the kind of realist I like to read and he's had a profound effect on me and not just intellectually. His writing has forced me to reexamine and change some of my habits.

Have to urinate. Again → no immediate pain but have to keep watch.

6:00 a.m. No pain after sleeping.

A lot of people who read literature go around judging whole groups of people filtered through the prejudice of some idea rather than judging what they see in the light of the present moment. Literature manufactures many a snob.
I don't mean to demean others' employments and enjoyments. My own life pressures me with special problems. In this world, ignorance is punished no matter how good the intentions are. In today's society, dreams are turning to nightmares.

MARCH 27TH, 1982
The only reaction to such ignorance is silence.

Articles in *Britannica* "Science, History of," "Science, Philosophy of," and "Nature, Philosophy of"

I have no money and few people are interested in what I have to say, so I read and reflect.

We maim each other by each our own limitations.

I can only be as much as another will allow me to be.

Read *You Can Quit Smoking in 14 Days* by Walter S. Ross. Resolved to become a nonsmoker.

MARCH 28TH, 1982
Resolved to smoke one cigarette every hour until I'm able to quit completely.

Have been able to smoke only one cigarette an hour for the past five hours.

Read *Towards a Self-Managed Life Style* by Williams and Long.

MARCH 31, 1982
Terry brought over some cake. I ate it but not feeling well.

APRIL 1, 1982
All of us are born with a principle which must come to fruition as a necessity. Our very genes unwind and wrap us up in a drama stronger than ourselves, even against our will and best intentions. I believe that there is a God and that there is a fate for each one of us. This God, I believe, knows our being down to the very chromosomes and knows our fears and why, and the share that others have in it, and takes that into account.

Age is a matter of the soul not the body.
I've known innocents seventy years old.

Delbridge reads to a packed house opening night of Rubber City Jazz and Blues Festival. This is his first performance since 1968, when he was a lead actor in the Morehouse-Spelman Players. Still image from *Tell It Like It Is*.

Delbridge receives accolades following a powerful performance at E. J. Thomas Hall in Akron. *Photo by Cameron Kaglic*.

A trucker, a poet, and a songwriter. Kevin Tucker, Walter Delbridge, and Kate Tucker. *Photo by Cameron Kaglic.*

Delbridge smiles for the camera. *Photo by Miriam Bennett.*

Acknowledgments

All photos courtesy of Red Valise Recordings from the *Tell It Like It Is* documentary film project.

"Jazz Coltrane Sings" was originally published in *We Speak as Liberators* by Orde Coombs (Dodd, Mead & Co., 1970.)

"Chinese River Prophet Song," "This the Poet as I See," and "The Metaphorical Egress" were first published in *Understanding the New Black Poetry: Black Speech and Black Music as Poetic References* by Stephen Evangelist Henderson (William and Morrow, 1973.)

"Letter to the National Institute of Mental Health" first appeared in part in "Isolation and Intellect—A Letter and Selected Works by Walter K. Delbridge." *Schizophrenia Bulletin* 43, no. 3 (May 1, 2017): 476–477.

Special thanks to Oxford University Press and Dr. William Carpenter, Editor-in-Chief of *Schizophrenia Bulletin*, for bringing Walter Delbridge's first-hand account to light. Thank you, Dr. Sohee Park of Vanderbilt University, for your open-hearted interest in Delbridge's experience, and for your lifelong research expanding the way we understand schizophrenia, its relationship to creativity, and the potential for recovery.

Gratitude to Leslie Stoyer and Ron Rhett, co-directors of the National Alliance on Mental Illness Summit County, to Robert Stokes, Michael Gaffney, Kimberly Meals, Lacy Vitko, Eileen Schwartz, and Shannon Jones of Community Support Services for your dedication and participation in Delbridge's comeback. Special thanks to the late Dr. Fred Frese, and to Elyn Saks of USC Gould School of Law for bearing courageous witness to your own experiences with schizophrenia, and for welcoming Delbridge into the conversation.

Thank you Courtney and Carter Little, Caroline Little Degenaars, and Nancy Hearon of the Charles Jacobs Foundation for your faith and vision.

This book came about in the midst of making the documentary, *Tell It Like It Is*, on the life and work of Walter K. Delbridge, so we give utmost gratitude to the ongoing and loving work of Joanna Tucker, Miriam Bennett, Jessie English, and Sarah Jane Holbrook.

Thank you, Elizabeth Meadows, Jay Clayton, and Kimberly Kane of Curb Center for Arts, Enterprise and Public Policy at Vanderbilt, and Jennifer Faye of Vanderbilt University Cinema and Media Arts for believing in Delbridge's story and summoning great minds to help in the telling, including Riley Beal, Basil Dababneh, Jonathan Tari, Christopher Hornbuckle, Stacy Horton, Karina Schechter, and Karl Schreiner.

Jordan Morgan, thank you for spending hours with me on a back porch in Nashville poring over handwritten manuscripts, envisioning the future. Thank you, Katelyn Meehan, for your synchronicity in approaching research, relationship, and the collective consciousness we all share as collaborators. And thank you, Don Pavlish, for your editorial eye, so kindly focused.

Many thanks to Eric Feigenbaum and Jessie English of Remedial Media for endless conversations on the direction of the project—your insight and friendship are gold.

Angelbert Metoyer, thank you for giving form and color to what cannot be known or told.

To the community of Akron, the librarians of Summit County, The Nightlight Cinema, and especially to Theron Brown, Rubber City Jazz and Blues Festival, Tony Troppe, BluJazz+, and to the venerable Jon Miller and The University of Akron Press, thank you for recognizing our living legend and welcoming him back to his rightful home.

Joanna Tucker, thank you for being a thoughtful barometer and steady support for all of us in this creative journey.

And finally we give thanks to the now-defunct Borders Books and Music for bringing together a trucker and a poet. And to that trucker, I say, "Dad, you sure know how to make a friend. Thank you for introducing us to Walter."

This the Poet... *Photo by Miriam Bennett*

Notes

1. "The single most frequent cause for black rejection [in the draft] was 'mental deficiency.'" Paul T. Murray, "Blacks and the Draft," *Journal of Black Studies* 2, no. 1 (September 1971): 57–75, doi:10.1177/002193477100200104.

"The evidence of bias in diagnosis underscored a robust phenomenon in African American mental health. For more than two decades, researchers have documented that African Americans have higher than expected rates of diagnosed schizophrenia." F. M. Baker and Carl C. Bell, "Issues in the Psychiatric Treatment of African Americans," *Psychiatric Services* 50, no. 3 (March 1999): 362–368, doi:10.1176/ps.50.3.362.

2. Most notably Kimberly W. Benston, *Performing Blackness: Enactments of African-American Modernism* (Taylor and Francis, 2013).

3. *Afrofuturism Is More Than Just "Black Sci Fi," It's a Nuanced Black Future, Inverse*, Video, Inverse Original, March 10, 2018, 3:07, www.inverse.com/article/42024-afrofuturism-is-not-just-black-sci-fi.

4. *Space is the Place,* directed by John Coney (1974; San Francisco, CA: North American Star System, Rhapsody Films, 1993), all media.

5. Ytasha L. Womack, *Afrofuturism: The World of Black Sci-Fi and Fantasy Culture* (Lawrence Hill Books, 2013).

6. Jonathan Metzl, *The Protest Psychosis: How Schizophrenia Became a Black Disease* (Beacon Press, 2011).

7. Walter Bromberg and Franck Simon. "The 'Protest' Psychosis," *Archives of General Psychiatry* 19, no. 2 (1968): 155–160, doi:10.1001/archpsyc.1968 .01740080027005.

8. Rutgers University, "African-Americans more likely to be misdiagnosed with schizophrenia, study finds: The study suggests a bias in misdiagnosing

blacks with major depression and schizophrenia." *ScienceDaily*, March 21, 2019, www.sciencedaily.com/releases/2019/03/190321130300.htm.

9. "Racism has always been a dominant factor in the selection of black draftees. [...] During the Korean War and again in the Vietnam War, blacks again have been overrepresented in the draft calls." Paul T. Murray, "Blacks and the Draft," *Journal of Black Studies* 2, no. 1 (1971): 57–75, doi:10.1177/002193 477100200104.

"During the Vietnam War African Americans faced a much greater chance of being on the front-line, and consequently a much higher casualty rate. In 1965 alone African-Americans represented almost 25 percent of those killed in action." "African-Americans in Combat | History Detectives," *PBS*, www.pbs.org/opb/historydetectives/feature/african-americans-in-combat/.

"Of the 246,000 men recruited under Project 100,000 between October 1966 and June 1969, 41% were black, although black Americans represented only 11% of the US population." James Maycock, "War within War," *The Guardian*, September 15, 2001, www.theguardian.com/theguardian/2001/sep/15/weekend7.weekend3.

10. "Researchers have documented notable differences between African Americans and Whites in rates of involuntary civil commitment." Kenneth P. Lindsey and Gordon L. Paul, "Involuntary Commitments to Public Mental Institutions: Issues Involving the Overrepresentation of Blacks and Assessment of Relevant Functioning," *Psychological Bulletin* 106, no. 2 (1989): 171–183, doi:10.1037/0033-2909.106.2.171.

"In particular, African Americans are disproportionately diagnosed with Schizophrenia with estimates ranging from three to five times more likely in receiving such a diagnosis [...] Barnes researched 2311 persons having a single admission to a state psychiatric hospital with a Schizophrenia diagnosis during an eight-year period. The researcher found that African Americans were four times more likely than Euro-Americans to receive a Schizophrenia diagnosis. Four years later, Barnes explored 2,404 persons admitted to Midwestern state psychiatric hospitals, finding that race was the strongest predictor of an admission diagnosis of Schizophrenia after controlling for the influence of other demographic variables." Schwartz, Robert C, and David M Blankenship, "Racial Disparities in Psychotic Disorder Diagnosis: A Review of Empirical Literature," *World Journal of Psychiatry*, Baishideng Publishing (December 22, 2014), www.ncbi.nlm.nih.gov/pmc/articles/PMC4274585/.

11. Andy Lewis, "Samuel L. Jackson: How I Became an Usher at Martin Luther King Jr.'s Funeral (guest column)," *The Hollywood Reporter*, April 3,

2018, www.hollywoodreporter.com/news/samuel-l-jackson-how-i-became
-an-usher-at-martin-luther-king-jrs-funeral-guest-column-1099033.

12. Betty Medsger, "Just Being Black Was Enough to Get Yourself Spied on
by J. Edgar Hoover's FBI," *The Nation*, June 29, 2015, www.thenation.com/
article/archive/just-being-black-was-enough-get-yourself-spied-j-edgar
-hoovers-fbi/.

13. D. Scot Miller, "Afrosurreal Manifesto: Black Is the New black—a
21st-Century Manifesto." *Black Camera* 5, no. 1 (Fall 2013): 113–117, *Project
MUSE.*

14. Shawn Mishak (June 22, 2020), "Filmmaker Traces the Tragic, Unortho-
dox Story of Akron Poet and Philosopher Walter Delbridge," https://www.
clevescene.com/scene-and-heard/archives/2020/06/22/filmmaker-traces-
the-tragic-unorthodox-story-of-akron-poet-and-philosopher-walter
-delbridge.

15. As printed in *We Speak as Liberators: Young Black Poets,* edited by Orde
Coombs (Dodd, Mead & Co., 1970).

16. Stephen Henderson, *Understanding the New Black Poetry: Black Speech
and Black Music as Poetic References* (William & Morrow, 1973). Henderson
was one of Delbridge's English professors at Morehouse.

17. Walter Dancy was born not in Tuskegee, but in Birmingham, Alabama,
on April 24, 1946. He spent his childhood in Tuskegee and moved to Akron
at age eleven.

18. Written in a birthday card to Kate Tucker, April 2012.

19. At the time of this publication, there remains a great deal of handwritten
work to transcribe, including April through December of the 1982 journals.
It is my hope that others will join in the ongoing exploration of Delbridge's
writings.

20. The actual quote reads: "Civilization is in a race between education and
catastrophe. Let us learn the truth and spread it as far and wide as our
circumstances allow. For the truth is the greatest weapon we have."

21. "He was right" written in the margins in Delbridge's handwriting.

22. Paraphrase of 1 Corinthians 2:14, "But the natural man receiveth not the
things of the Spirit of God: for they are foolishness unto him: neither can he
know them, because they are spiritually discerned."

23. Paraphrase from a letter John Keats wrote to his sister and brother, in
which he refers to the world as a "vale of Soul-making."

Bibliography

"African-Americans in Combat | History Detectives." *Public Broadcasting Service*, www.pbs.org/opb/historydetectives/feature/african-americans-in-combat/.

Baker, F. M., and Carl C. Bell. "Issues in the Psychiatric Treatment of African Americans." *Psychiatric Services* 50, no. 3 (1999): 362–368, doi:10.1176/ps.50.3.362.

Baldwin, James. *Nobody Knows My Name*. Vintage Books, 1993.

Balfour, Arthur James, and Joseph Needham. *Science, Religion and Reality*. Kennikat Press, 1970.

Barbour, Ian G. *Issues in Science and Religion*. SCM Press, 1972.

Bartlett, John, and Nathan Haskell Dole. *Familiar Quotations: A Collection of Passages, Phrases, and Proverbs* (10th Ed., rev. and enl.). Blue Ribbon Books, 1919.

Becker, Ernest. *The Denial of Death*. Free Press, 1973.

Bell, Eric Temple. *Men of Mathematics*. Simon & Schuster, 2008.

Bennett, John Godolphin. "Creative Thinking." In *Creative Thinking*. Coombe Springs Press, 1975.

Benston, Kimberley W. *Performing Blackness: Enactments of African-American Modernism*. Taylor and Francis, 2013.

Bibby, C. The Essence of T. H. Huxley: *Selections from His Writings*. Macmillan & Co., 1967.

Bloom, Bernard L. *Community Mental Health: A Historical and Critical Analysis*. General Learning Press, 1973.

Bolam, David W., and James Lewis Henderson. *Art and Belief*. Schocken Books, 1970.

Bromberg, Walter, and Franck Simon. "The 'Protest' Psychosis." *Archives of General Psychiatry* 19, no. 2 (1968): 155–160, doi:10.1001/archpsyc.1968 .01740080027005.

Bryson, Lyman. *An Outline of Man's Knowledge of the Modern World.* McGraw-Hill, 1966.

Buscaglia, Leo F. *Personhood: The Art of Being Fully Human.* Fawcett Columbine, 1982.

Chardin, Pierre Teilhard de. *Activation of Energy.* Harcourt, Inc., 1978.

Chardin, Pierre Teilhard de. *Human Energy.* Harcourt Brace Jovanovich, 1979.

Coney, John, dir. *Space is the Place.* 1974; San Francisco, CA: North American Star System, Rhapsody Films, 1993, all media.

Coombs, Orde. *We Speak as Liberators: Young Black Poets.* Dodd, Mead & Co., 1970.

Delbridge, Walter K., and Kate Tucker. "Isolation and Intellect—A Letter and Selected Works by Walter K. Delbridge." *Schizophrenia Bulletin* 43, no. 3 (May 1, 2017): 476–477, doi:10.1093/schbul/sbw150.

Deloria, Vine. *The Metaphysics of Modern Existence.* Fulcrum Publishing, 1979.

Dewey, John. *Human Nature and Conduct.* Carlton House, 1922.

Dunaway, Philip, et al. *A Treasury of the World's Great Diaries.* Doubleday, 1957.

Duncan, R., and M. Weston-Smith. *The Encyclopaedia of Ignorance.* Pergamon Press, 1977.

Einstein, Albert. *Living Philosophies.* Ams Press, 1931.

Ferguson, Marilyn. *Aquarian Conspiracy.* Houghton Mifflin, 1981.

Fraser, J. T. *Of Time, Passion and Knowledge: Reflections on the Strategy of Existence.* Princeton University Press, 1975.

Garcia, John David. *The Moral Society: A Rational Alternative to Death.* Julian Press, 1971.

Groch, Judith. *The Right to Create.* Little, Brown, 1970.

Hall, Calvin S. *A Primer of Freudian Psychology.* The New American Library of World Literature, 1961.

Henderson, Stephen Evangelist. *Understanding the New Black Poetry: Black Speech and Black Music as Poetic References.* William and Morrow Company, 1973.

Hills, Christopher B., et al. *The Rise of the Phoenix: Universal Government by Nature's Laws.* Common Ownership Press, 1979.

Hills, Christopher. *Nuclear Evolution: Discovery of the Rainbow Body.* University of the Trees Press, 1979.

Hogben, Lancelot Thomas. *Science for the Citizen*. Allen and Unwin, 1957.

Horizon: A Magazine of the Arts, May 1961.

Huxley, Aldous. *Tomorrow and Tomorrow and Tomorrow, and Other Essays*. Harper, 1956.

Huxley, Julian Sorell. *Religion without Revelation*. Watts, 1967.

Isherwood, Christopher. *Vedanta for Modern Man*. Mentor Books, 1972.

Jones, Bessie Zaban. *The Golden Age of Science: Thirty Portraits of the Giants of 19th-Century Science*. Simon and Schuster, in Cooperation with the Smithsonian Institution, Washington, 1966.

Keyes, Ken. *Handbook to Higher Consciousness*. Cornucopia, 1974.

Komenský Jan Amos, and Matthew Spinka. *The Labyrinth of the World and the Paradise of the Heart That Is a Bright Portrayal Showing That in This World and in Its Works There Is Nothing but Confusion and Staggering, Floundering and Drudgery*. University of Michigan, 1972.

Kovel, Joel. *The Age of Desire: Case Histories of a Radical Psychoanalyst*. Pantheon Books, 1981.

Krutch, Joseph Wood. *If You Don't Mind My Saying So: Essays on Man and Nature*. William Sloane Associates, 1964.

Lewis, Andy. "Samuel L. Jackson: How I Became an Usher at Martin Luther King Jr.'s Funeral (Guest Column)." *The Hollywood Reporter*, April 3, 2018, www.hollywoodreporter.com/news/samuel-l-jackson-how-i -became-an-usher-at-martin-luther-king-jrs-funeral-guest-column -1099033.

Lindsey, Kenneth P., and Gordon L. Paul. "Involuntary Commitments to Public Mental Institutions: Issues Involving the Overrepresentation of Blacks and Assessment of Relevant Functioning." *Psychological Bulletin* 106, no. 2 (1989): 171–183, doi:10.1037/0033-2909.106.2.171.

Lonergan, Bernard J. *Insight: A Study of Human Understanding*. New York, 1958.

Lovejoy, Arthur Oncken. *Reflections on Human Nature*. Johns Hopkins Press, 1961.

Maycock, James. "War within War." *The Guardian*, Guardian News and Media, September 15, 2001, www.theguardian.com/theguardian/2001/ sep/15/weekend7.weekend3.

Marden, Orison Swett. *Architects of Fate: Or, Steps to Success and Power*. Project Gutenberg, 1897.

Medsger, Betty. "Just Being Black Was Enough to Get Yourself Spied on by J. Edgar Hoover's FBI." *The Nation*, June 29, 2015. www.thenation.com/ article/archive/just-being-black-was-enough-get-yourself-spied-j-edgar- hoovers-fbi/.

Metzl, Jonathan. *The Protest Psychosis: How Schizophrenia Became a Black Disease*. Beacon, 2011.

Miller, D. Scot. "Afrosurreal Manifesto: Black Is the New black—a 21st-Century Manifesto." *Black Camera* 5 no. 1 (2013): 113–117.

Murchie, Guy. *The Seven Mysteries of Life: An Exploration in Science and Philosophy*. Houghton Mifflin, 1978.

Murray, Paul T. "Blacks and the Draft." *Journal of Black Studies* 2, no. 1 (1971): 57–75, doi:10.1177/002193477100200104.

Needleman, Jacob. *A Sense of the Cosmos: The Encounter of Modern Science and Ancient Truth*. Dutton, 1976.

Nicoll, Maurice. *Psychological Commentaries on the Teaching of G. I. Gurdjieff and P. D. Ouspensky*. Vincent Harris, 1952.

Nordby, Vernon J., and Calvin S. Hall. *A Guide to Psychologists and Their Concepts*. W. H. Freeman, 1974.

Pascal, Blaise. *Pensées*. Penguin Classics, 1966.

Patterson, Cecil Holden. *Theories of Counseling and Psychotherapy*. Harper & Row, 1986.

Pervin, Lawrence A. *Personality: Theory, Assessment, and Research*. Wiley, 1980.

Powys, John Cowper. *A Philosophy of Solitude*. Simon & Schuster, 1933.

Randall, John Herman. *Readings in Philosophy*. Barnes and Noble Books, 1972.

Reik, Theodor. *Listening with the Third Ear*. Farrar, Straus, 1949.

Rideau Émile. *Teilhard De Chardin: A Guide to His Thought*. Collins, 1967.

Ross, Walter Sanford. *You Can Quit Smoking in 14 Days*. Berkley Pub. Corp., 1976.

Rutgers University. "African-Americans more likely to be misdiagnosed with schizophrenia, study finds: The study suggests a bias in misdiagnosing blacks with major depression and schizophrenia." ScienceDaily, March 21, 2019. www.sciencedaily.com/releases/2019/03/190321130300.htm.

Santayana, George. *The Philosophy of Santayana*. Scribner, 1953.

Sappenfield, Bert Reese. *Personality Dynamics an Integrative Psychology of Adjustment*. Knopf, 1954.

Schindler, John A. *How to Live 365 Days of the Year*. Prentice-Hall, 1973.

Schwartz, Robert C, and David M Blankenship. "Racial Disparities in Psychotic Disorder Diagnosis: A Review of Empirical Literature." *World Journal of Psychiatry*, Baishideng Publishing Group (December 22, 2014). www.ncbi.nlm.nih.gov/pmc/articles/PMC4274585/.

Soleri, Paolo. *Fragments: A Selection from the Sketchbooks of Paolo Soleri: The Tiger Paradigm-Paradox*. Harper & Row, 1981.

Soleri, Paolo. *The Omega Seed: An Eschatological Hypothesis*. Anchor Press/ Doubleday, 1981.

Tiedt, Sidney W. "Creativity." *Creativity*. General Learning Press, 1976.

The New Encyclopaedia Britannica. Encyclopaedia Britannica, 1980.

Toynbee, Arnold. *An Historians Approach to Religion*. Oxford University Press, 1979.

Video, Inverse Original, director. *Afrofuturism Is More Than Just "Black Sci Fi," It's a Nuanced Black Future. Inverse*, March 10, 2018. www.inverse. com/article/42024-afrofuturism-is-not-just-black-sci-fi.

Voronoff, Serge. *From Cretin to Genius*. Alliance Book Corporation, 1941.

Wells, H. G. *The Time Machine*. Dent, 1935.

White, Joseph L. *The Creation of a God: The Struggle of Life for Perfection in a Spiritual World of Science*. White, 1975.

Whyte, Lancelot Law. *The Next Development in Man*. New American Library of World Literature, 1948.

Wieman, Henry Nelson. *Methods of Private Religious Living*. Macmillan, 1938.

Williams, Robert L, and James D. Long. *Toward a Self-Managed Life Style*. Houghton Mifflin, 1975.

Womack, Ytasha L. *Afrofuturism the World of Black Sci-Fi and Fantasy Culture*. Lawrence Books, 2013.

Yankelovich, Daniel, and William Barrett. *Ego and Instinct: The Psychoanalytic View of Human Nature—Revised*. Vintage Books, 1971.

Young, J. Z. *An Introduction to the Study of Man*. Oxford University Press, 1974.

Having studied at Harvard, Yale, and Morehouse, **Walter Delbridge** was on his way to the Sorbonne as one of the first African Americans to receive a Ford Foundation scholarship, when a diagnosis of schizophrenia changed the trajectory of his life. While institutionalized in a psychiatric hospital, his poetry was published alongside the likes of Langston Hughes, Lead Belly, Gwendolyn Brooks, and Audre Lorde in the renowned anthology *Understanding the New Black Poetry* and in Orde Coomb's *We Speak As Liberators*. He continued to write in isolation and in 2017, Oxford University Press published new poetry from Delbridge, along with his letter to the National Institute of Mental Health, in their flagship journal *Schizophrenia Bulletin*. Now seventy-six, he spends day and night among stacks of books in his apartment in Middlebury, Akron's oldest neighborhood.

Kate Tucker is a writer, artist, and producer born and raised in Akron, Ohio. As a singer-songwriter, she's released five albums, two EPs, and twenty-three music videos. Her production work includes books, films, podcasts, fashion editorials, and art exhibitions. Tucker holds a B.A. in English and French from The University of Akron, and she's guest lectured at Vanderbilt and Belmont Universities. Having recently returned to Akron after living in Paris, Seattle, New York, and Nashville, Tucker is working with Delbridge on the documentary film, *Tell It Like It Is*, centered on his life and work.